THE ECONOMICS OF NATIONAL SECURITY

VOLUME II

BASIC ECONOMICS
Refresher Notes

Andrew J. Kress, Ph. D.

INDUSTRIAL COLLEGE OF THE ARMED FORCES
WASHINGTON, D. C.

Reprint 1957

Reprint April 1958

Third Printing
February 1959

Fourth Printing
October 1959

Fifth Printing
February 1960

Acknowledgments

The College is indebted to Dr. Lester V. Chandler, Gordon S. Rentschler, Professor of Economics, Princeton University, author of chapter XIII, taken from Chandler and Wallace, *Economic Mobilization and Stabilization*, Henry Holt and Company, Inc., New York. It is used by permission of the publisher.

Industrial College of the Armed Forces.

Washington, D. C.
December 1957

CONTENTS

FIGURES

TABLES

I

THE METHODS AND TOOLS OF ECONOMICS

FACT AND FICTION REGARDING ECONOMICS

Economists are constantly subjected to a great deal of good-natured hazing. They are told that economic theory is only common sense made difficult. However, common sense remains the most uncommon of senses. Everyone deals with the practicalities of economics in one form or another, day in and day out.

One reads that the law of supply and demand has been repealed; that the classical economist deluded himself with his analysis of one element in a formula, other things being equal, though everyone now knows that other things never remain equal; that pure competition is a mere textbook idiosyncracy; and that there is only competition by industries. One hears that little competition exists in industry and that prices are purely administered; that the old idea of *laissez faire* has to be given up in these modern days or that it never existed anyway; that businessmen aim to maximize their profits or that they are powerless to do so; that Keynes' ideas pertained only to a depression economy or that they will really take hold in an inflationary period. It is said that economic forecasting based on reliable statistics will soon be dependable. The mere existence of reliable statistics, however, cannot guarantee that the required legislative steps and the necessary appropriation actions will follow.

The truth is that there is still competition in business, more in some industries than in others. There is competition in price, in quality, in service, in advertising, and in salesmanship. A few markets still approximate *pure and perfect competition;* in many more *differentiation of the product* achieves competition. Some businesses are easier to enter into than others, and there are varying degrees of price collusion and agreements among producers. The opportunity to substitute one type of product for another is in itself a check on administered pricing. We can shorten lengthy, old-time explanations of supply and demand, but we cannot dispense with these explanations altogether.

The industrial world of today is a very different one from that upon which the classical economist looked. The deductive logic of the classicist may have restricted economic discussion to the adept, but the methodology is still useful. From time to time various schools of economics have appeared. Each has its own approach or its preferred way of going about the study of economic theory and phenomena. These approaches include in addition to the deductive, the historical, descriptive, theoretical, and statistical schools. Actually the economist uses each of those approaches at various times.

The historical approach is of course a chronological one. The descriptive school details the features of economic institutions, such as the corporation, the trade association, and the labor union. The theoretical approach is devoted to analyzing the economic system, seeking to discover laws, theories, and principles. At the moment all economists are concerned with statistical procedures as a basis for economic forecasting. Currently some economists are enthusiastic over "model building" (argument from assumptions). Altogether, interest in economics was never at a higher peak than it is today.

ECONOMICS AS A SCIENCE

Much debate as to whether economics is a science can be avoided by a few definitions and classifications. If we divide the sciences generally into two main divisions, the natural sciences and the social sciences, and carefully define each classification, we do not need to worry whether or how much they overlap, whether they are similar or dissimilar. Perhaps they share only some of the same research methods.

The natural sciences include such subjects as chemistry, physics, and biology. Research personnel devote their energies to the study of natural phenomena and endeavor to discover natural law. They use laboratory experiment as a vital part of the learning processes. It is probably correct to say that engineers use scientific method in what is basically an art, the daily application of scientific laws and discoveries to practical ends.

The social sciences deal with the various phases of human organizations and activities. Economics has to do with human wants; sociology, with the working relationships growing out of human congregation in groups; and psychology, with human emotions. When the social scientist speaks of his discipline as a science, he means only that he is concerned with a connected body of observed facts which have been systematically classified and which he deals with as scientifically as the materials permit. He tries to discover general laws under trustworthy methods within the domain of the individual discipline. For the social scientist, a science is a systematized and classified body of knowledge of things gained through a study of their causes, frequency and traits.

Society's respect for human life and human personality forbids the application of the same techniques to social phenomena as the natural scientist applies to nonhuman phenomena. He cannot put people in test tubes and dissolve or combine them for experimental purposes. The social-science laboratories are nevertheless significant in the enlargement of social knowledge. The application of scientific method to human problems is occupying the attention of many well-trained persons. The current attempts at economic forecasting furnish an example of the application of scholarly methods. These efforts are in their infancy and encounter serious obstacles. There is a definite quality or characteristic in human beings which allows them to resist their environment. Sometimes they say "no" when the indicated answer is "yes." The prediction of mass conduct and even of the behavior of smaller groups enjoys some success, but it is still perilous to predict individual conduct.

METHODS OF ECONOMICS

The methods of the several schools of economics have been mentioned. An older approach to ecomonic analysis began with a study of the economic motives and the economic behavior of a single individual. It progressed to a study of the motive and behavior of the individual firm, thence to that of an entire industry, and finally to a consideration of the working of the economic system as a whole. This method of studying the total economy by progressing from the individual to the whole is sometimes known as *micro-economics*.

The newer approach examines the economic system by observing its operation as a whole and the overall conditions of production; national income, total demand, supply, consumption, investment and savings, as well as total employment. Then it works backward to observe the contribution of a single industry to total production, moves backward further to observe the contribution of the individual firm to its own single industry and finally the relation of the individual person to the individual business. This approach is known as *macro-economics* and as the *economics of aggregates*.

The simple fact is that neither approach is complete in itself; both must be understood and related to each other. The overall production of goods and services is based on multiple decisions, on the decisions of many individual businessmen, on thousands of decisions by individual persons, and on many decisions by the Government. Some of these decisions will result in the contraction of output, and some will result in expansion thereof, some will close old businesses, and some will open new ones. We cannot understand the economic system by attention to aggregates or totals only. We must also examine the economic conduct of individuals, of individual firms, and of individual industries.

MODERN ECONOMIC TOOLS

THE NATION'S INCOME: EXPENDITURES AND SAVINGS

The Nation's income, expenditures, and savings can be represented by a series of accounts showing total receipts and total expenditures for consumers, business, and Government. Combined receipts, which include consumer disposable income, gross retained earnings of business, and Government receipts, must equal the combined expenditures—consumption expenditures, gross private domestic investment plus net foreign investment, and Government expenditures. Statistics and estimates covering these accounts in several subcategories are published monthly by the United States Department of Commerce. Trends in the business cycle can be traced through changes in these statistics.[1]

INPUT-OUTPUT ANALYSIS

Interindustry economics, or input-output analysis, is a method that attempts to present statistically the relatively stable pattern of the flow of goods and services among the elements of our economy. The Division of Interindustry Economics, Bureau of Labor Statistics, U. S. Department of Labor, began the production in 1948 of tables showing in summary form the distribution of the value of all output in the United States in 1947 for 50 industries, by both industry of origin (production) and industry of destination (use). All transactions involving the sale of products of services within an economy during a given period are arranged in a square indicating simultaneously the sectors making and the sectors receiving delivery. All of the 50 industries are listed down the left side of the table and also across the top of the table. Each horizontal row shows the sales made by one economic sector to every other sector, and each vertical column shows what one economic sector purchased from every other sector.

Thus, Agriculture and Fisheries, number 1 in the list of industries at the left, sold (or used) $10,856 million to the industry, Agriculture and Fisheries. This amount represents its output used by the industry itself. It sold to Food and Kindred Products $15,048 million. That is, the output of Agriculture and Fisheries which was used by Food and Kindred Products was $15,048 million. In like manner the output of Agriculture and Fisheries used by Tobacco Manufactures and Textile Mill Products was respectively $783 million and $2,079 million. Thus, the total output of Agriculture and Fisheries was $44,263 million. It was used (purchased) by the industries listed at the top of the chart in the amounts shown in the first row, under the respective industries. Likewise, each industry listed at

[1] See chapter VIII, page 53.

the left produced and sold to each industry listed at the top, the amount in the square where the two said industry spaces intersect. For example, Chemicals' (left) output used by Iron and Steel (top) was $99 million.

In summary, each industry listed at the left had an output equal to that shown in the last column, "Total Gross Output." How was this "Total Gross Output" of Chemicals, for example, of $14,050 million disposed of? Follow this row from left to right and see how much of Chemicals each industry listed at the top bought or used. For example, the Apparel industry used $142 million.

A detailed and accurate analysis of how the output of any industry was used or sold is useful to that industry. It reveals the industries on which it is dependent and the amount of that dependence. Any actual or proposed change in one of these user industries is reflected in the industry considered and may suggest an increase or decrease in the industry's production plans. For many important national economic problems, it is essential to establish consistent connections between demand for finished products, on the one hand, and on the other, the implications of this demand for production, employment, capacity utilization, and resource use levels of industries that may be remotely involved. For example, a decision to produce additional munitions (which are end products) will affect not just the industries that assemble and deliver these items, but also in some way virtually every other industry in the economy as well. The question as to whether any comprehensive addition to current schedules of demand will produce overloads, in terms of manpower, capacity, or resource limitations as critical points, cannot be answered unless some consistent connection can be found between an addition to the demand schedule and its impact throughout the economic system.

THE FLOW-OF-FUNDS SYSTEM

The Board of Governors of the Federal Reserve System announced in its *Bulletin* for October 1955 the inauguration of a new accounting record designed to picture the flow of funds through the major sectors of the national economy. The Board believes that insight into the functioning of an economy can be greatly enhanced by casting available information into a systematic and comprehensive structure of economic accounts. Application of accounting methods to the organization of economic data aids in both collection and interpretation of economic knowledge. It highlights gaps in the basic statistics and clarifies interrelations among the parts of the structure. In a highly interdependent economy, credit and monetary developments necessarily play a strategic role.

In this system, records of the flow of funds are organized into detailed statements of the sources and uses of funds for each of 10 major groups or sectors into which the economy is divided, table 2. Transactions of each individual sector in the flow of funds accounts are classified into nonfinancial and financial categories. For any given year, a chart with columns across the top for each of the major sectors and with the nonfinancial and financial categories listed on the left side will show at a glance the participation of each sector in each group of transactions for that year. Comparison of annual charts for a series of years will indicate trends in the economy.

ECONOMIC INDICATORS

The U. S. Departments of Labor and Commerce and the Federal Reserve System gather and publish extensive figures each month dealing with labor, manpower, wages, construction, commerce, and finance. Joint Resolution of the Senate and House of Representatives, approved 23 June 1949, authorized the Joint Committee on the Economic Report to issue a monthly publication entitled *Economic Indicators* for official distribution and public sale. This report is actually prepared for the Joint Economic Committee by the Council of Economic Advisers. The council issues its own monthly reports in graphic form. These reports are based on statistics of the three agencies named above, and cover Total Output, Income, and Spending; Employment, Unemployment, and Wages; Production and Business Activity; Prices; Currency, Credit, and Security Markets; and Federal Finance. Each graph is preceded by one or two short sentences interpreting trends and changes in relation to a previous period.[2]

[2] See chapter IX, page 63.

Table 2. Summary of Flow-of-Funds Accounts for 1953

S = Sources of Funds, U = Uses of Funds

(Annual flows, in billions of dollars)

Sectors	Consumer		Business: Corporate		Business: Non-corporate		Business: Farm		Government: Federal		Government: St. and loc.		Financial institutions: Banking		Financial institutions: Insurance		Financial institutions: Other		Rest of the world		Total	
Transactions	S	U	S	U	S	U	S	U	S	U	S	U	S	U	S	U	S	U	S	U	S	U
Nonfinancial																						
A Payroll	195.5	2.7	....	118.7	....	30.0	....	2.6	....	19.0	....	13.5	....	1.9	....	2.6	....	4.4	....	*	195.5	195.5
B Receipts from and payments on investment	59.4	16.3	9.7	20.0	17.5	40.0	1.1	13.0	1.0	5.5	.8	1.0	6.2	2.1	3.5	.3	1.7	1.5	.5	1.9	101.4	101.4
C Insurance and grants	23.9	22.7	1.3	12.2	1.0	3.0	.4	.4	7.5	14.4	11.9	11.7	*	.3	29.0	16.7	5.7	1.4	2.2	.3	82.8	83.0
D Taxes and tax refunds	2.6	40.9	.5	36.0	....	6.8	....	1.1	64.8	3.1	21.4	....	....	.8	....	.7	....	*	....	*	89.4	89.6
E Capital acquisitions	22.0	63.8	.2	26.7	1.5	6.0	.4	5.0	*	4.2	.1	7.8	....	.1	*	.2	....	2.1	....	....		
F *Net change in inventories*	....	....	....	*1.6*	....	*.9*	....	*.3*	....	....	....	....	....	....	....	....	....	....	....	....		
G *New fixed capital*	....	*39.4*	....	*24.9*	....	*5.1*	....	*4.6*	....	*4.2*	....	*7.2*	....	*.1*	....	*	....	*2.1*	....	....		
H *Other*	*22.0*	*24.4*	*.2*	*.2*	*1.5*	*	*.4*	....	*	*.1*	*.1*	*.5*	....	....	*	*.2*	....	....	....	....	820.9	819.5
I Purchases and sales of other goods and services	....	155.4	538.3	341.8	195.8	130.2	29.8	10.8	5.0	38.8	5.8	6.4	.8	.7	.5	3.4	4.9	3.0	15.8	14.3		
J **Total**	**303.4**	**301.8**	**550.0**	**555.3**	**215.9**	**215.9**	**31.7**	**32.8**	**78.4**	**85.1**	**40.0**	**40.4**	**7.0**	**5.9**	**33.0**	**23.9**	**12.3**	**12.4**	**18.4**	**16.5**	**1,290.0**	**1,290.0**
Financial																						
K Currency and deposits	....	4.4	....	.1	....	.4	....	*	....	−1.6	....	1.0	5.0	....	....	.2	....	.2	*	.3	5.0	5.0
L Federal obligations	....	.3	....	1.1	....	.6	....	....	5.2	....	....	1.8	....	.9	....	*	....	−.2	....	.6	5.2	5.1
M Mortgages	6.2	.6	1.3	....	1.8	.5	.4	....	....	.3	....	....	....	2.5	....	2.1	*	3.7	....	....	9.8	9.8
N Corporate securities and State and local obligations	....	3.2	6.7	.3	....	−.6	....	....	....	−.3	3.6	.3	.1	1.1	....	6.5	.4	.3	.1	.1	10.9	10.8
O Other	4.5	4.4	−.6	.1	1.6	2.3	.6	*	.1	.2	....	....	.2	1.4	.3	.2	4.5	.9	.6	1.4	11.8	10.8
P **Total**	**10.7**	**12.9**	**7.4**	**1.6**	**3.5**	**3.2**	**1.0**	*	**5.3**	**−1.4**	**3.6**	**3.0**	**5.2**	**5.8**	**.3**	**9.1**	**5.0**	**5.0**	**.6**	**2.3**	**42.6**	**41.5**
Q **Grand total**	**314.4**	**314.4**	**557.4**	**557.4**	**219.3**	**219.3**	**32.8**	**32.8**	**83.7**	**83.7**	**43.6**	**43.6**	**12.2**	**12.2**	**33.3**	**33.3**	**17.3**	**17.3**	**19.0**	**19.0**	**1,332.7**	**1,332.7**
Memoranda:																						
R GNP identifiable in J	....	215.1	....	29.5	....	6.9	....	6.9	....	57.9	....	24.4	....	1.4	....	*	....	10.7	....	−1.9	....	350.9
S Bank credit in P	3.5	....	.5	....	1.2	....	.6	....	.9	....	.7	....	*	6.9	....	....	−.1	....	−.2	....	6.9	6.9

*Less than 50 million dollars

[1]Financial sources of funds represent net changes in liabilities; financial uses of funds represent net changes in financial assets.

Table 1

INTERINDUSTRY FLOW OF GOODS AND SERVICES BY INDUSTRY OF ORIGIN AND DESTINATION, 1947

(All figures in millions of dollars)

INDUSTRY PURCHASING

INDUSTRY PRODUCING	1 AGRICULTURE & FISHERIES	2 FOOD & KINDRED PRODUCTS	3 TOBACCO MANUFACTURES	4 TEXTILE MILL PRODUCTS	5 APPAREL	6 LUMBER & WOOD PRODUCTS	7 FURNITURE & FIXTURES	8 PAPER & ALLIED PRODUCTS	9 PRINTING & PUBLISHING	10 CHEMICALS	11 PRODUCTS OF PETROLEUM & COAL	12 RUBBER PRODUCTS	13 LEATHER & LEATHER PRODUCTS	14 STONE, CLAY & GLASS PRODUCTS	15 IRON & STEEL	16 NONFERROUS METALS	17 PLUMBING & HEATING SUPPLIES	18 FABRICATED STRUCTURAL METAL PRODUCTS	19 OTHER FABRICATED METAL PRODUCTS	20 AGRIC'L, MINING & CONST. MACHINERY	21 METALWORKING MACHINERY	22 OTHER MACHINERY (except electric)	23 MOTORS & GENERATORS	24 RADIOS	25 OTHER ELECTRICAL MACHINERY
1 AGRICULTURE & FISHERIES	10,856	15,048	783	2,079	19	192	-	9	-	1,211	-	-	49	*	-	11	-	-	-	-	-	-	-	-	-
2 FOOD & KINDRED PRODUCTS	2,378	4,910	15	60	9	*	*	30	*	685	*	-	444	2	3	*	-	-	*	-	-	*	-	-	*
3 TOBACCO MANUFACTURES	-	-	828	-	-	-	-	-	-	1	-	-	-	-	-	-	-	-	-	-	-	-	-	-	-
4 TEXTILE MILL PRODUCTS	64	2	-	1,303	3,882	3	285	43	25	13	2	444	88	33	-	-	*	*	8	2	1	18	2	9	36
5 APPAREL	44	204	-	-	1,963	-	5	20	-	30	-	-	2	3	-	-	*	-	1	*	-	2	-	*	*
6 LUMBER & WOOD PRODUCTS	148	81	18	18	2	1,094	385	267	1	45	6	-	17	17	36	28	23	5	34	15	4	67	3	10	41
7 FURNITURE & FIXTURES	-	-	-	12	-	-	7	5	-	-	-	-	-	-	-	-	*	-	-	-	-	5	-	102	1
8 PAPER & ALLIED PRODUCTS	2	453	65	78	25	5	15	2,597	1,081	331	112	20	54	179	*	*	9	5	79	2	2	39	4	17	48
9 PRINTING & PUBLISHING	-	39	-	2	-	-	-	-	767	16	-	-	-	-	-	-	1	-	11	2	1	5	-	1	5
10 CHEMICALS	830	1,451	25	800	142	26	63	183	97	2,655	213	604	126	116	99	85	21	18	88	17	5	62	10	9	178
11 PRODUCTS OF PETROLEUM & COAL	457	58	*	30	5	74	1	63	3	325	4,829	12	2	50	846	49	7	3	12	9	4	24	1	2	18
12 RUBBER PRODUCTS	122	9	-	13	18	9	6	9	3	1	1	41	50	8	*	*	2	2	5	75	2	53	2	2	31
13 LEATHER & LEATHER PRODUCTS	-	-	-	2	53	4	7	-	4	-	-	-	1,037	-	-	-	*	*	1	3	11	7	*	*	1
14 STONE, CLAY & GLASS PRODUCTS	65	253	1	1	*	14	34	28	-	258	46	7	5	430	180	33	9	6	52	7	10	57	23	7	92
15 IRON & STEEL	6	2	-	-	1	10	97	-	-	5	6	14	1	23	3,982	33	172	553	1,374	532	143	930	118	13	196
16 NONFERROUS METALS	-	-	-	-	-	2	16	-	14	189	1	*	*	13	324	2,599	94	63	272	24	23	366	40	26	654
17 PLUMBING & HEATING SUPPLIES	-	-	-	-	-	-	-	-	-	-	-	-	-	-	15	-	39	41	7	-	-	35	1	-	32
18 FABRICATED STRUCTURAL METAL PRODUCTS	-	-	-	-	-	-	5	-	-	-	-	-	-	-	7	-	19	42	18	33	1	67	*	-	9
19 OTHER FABRICATED METAL PRODUCTS	83	543	15	*	6	35	132	17	1	130	78	12	16	4	24	4	72	90	213	93	67	326	28	63	211
20 AGRIC'L, MINING & CONST. MACHINERY	59	-	-	-	-	-	-	-	-	-	-	-	-	5	15	7	-	23	-	115	20	96	-	-	-
21 METALWORKING MACHINERY	-	-	-	-	-	-	-	-	-	-	-	-	-	-	8	7	6	9	53	51	57	90	7	6	19
22 OTHER MACHINERY (except electric)	-	13	-	35	21	14	11	14	35	1	5	-	-	2	27	4	110	43	41	307	68	565	50	2	82
23 MOTORS & GENERATORS	-	-	-	-	-	-	-	-	-	-	-	-	-	-	-	-	34	7	1	32	29	317	17	5	52
24 RADIOS	-	-	-	-	-	-	-	-	-	-	-	-	-	-	-	*	1	-	13	-	-	4	8	243	95
25 OTHER ELECTRICAL MACHINERY	-	-	-	-	-	-	-	-	-	1	-	-	-	7	8	46	53	9	125	22	16	158	57	165	350
26 MOTOR VEHICLES	111	3	-	-	-	1	-	-	-	-	*	-	-	1	*	*	-	-	32	24	7	*	-	-	12
27 OTHER TRANSPORTATION EQUIPMENT	10	-	-	-	-	-	-	*	-	1	*	*	-	*	2	1	-	-	-	-	-	-	*	-	-
28 PROFESSIONAL & SCIENTIFIC EQUIPMENT	-	-	-	-	-	-	2	6	32	13	-	-	-	1	*	-	34	3	3	1	2	36	2	3	9
29 MISCELLANEOUS MANUFACTURING	4	11	-	4	256	1	16	15	-	29	-	*	22	9	5	*	1	1	18	*	1	45	20	30	61
30 COAL, GAS & ELECTRIC POWER	61	193	4	105	36	24	18	123	29	188	556	37	15	204	242	104	13	15	52	23	14	68	8	6	39
31 RAILROAD TRANSPORTATION	440	548	21	94	60	143	54	224	68	287	270	36	36	145	423	100	19	37	77	44	12	100	11	13	50
32 OCEAN TRANSPORTATION	73	126	3	13	11	9	*	16	*	44	94	*	1	14	30	52	*	*	*	*	*	*	-	*	*
33 OTHER TRANSPORTATION	553	367	16	79	25	138	40	117	25	95	470	7	21	70	140	19	6	5	17	10	3	29	3	8	19
34 TRADE	1,360	418	38	228	369	60	60	176	31	173	19	55	57	52	216	140	36	54	110	51	22	183	18	34	83
35 COMMUNICATIONS	2	41	1	9	19	10	6	8	39	23	15	6	5	10	16	6	3	6	13	6	4	23	3	4	13
36 FINANCE & INSURANCE	238	145	1	20	24	77	18	18	23	18	125	7	7	46	44	14	6	14	19	11	7	32	7	9	23
37 RENTAL	2,393	91	2	25	96	19	17	26	61	34	-	10	19	18	36	21	4	10	20	6	6	32	2	9	19
38 BUSINESS SERVICES	8	533	98	71	97	19	57	22	58	424	42	21	49	11	25	5	16	10	25	12	11	64	3	25	32
39 PERSONAL & REPAIR SERVICES	368	119	*	3	3	42	4	4	20	11	13	1	1	31	3	3	1	4	3	2	1	5	*	*	1
40 MEDICAL, EDUC. & NONPROFIT ORG'S	-	-	-	-	-	-	-	-	-	-	-	-	-	-	-	-	-	-	-	-	-	-	-	-	-
41 AMUSEMENTS	-	-	-	-	-	-	-	-	-	-	-	-	-	-	-	-	-	-	-	-	-	-	-	-	-
42 SCRAP & MISCELLANEOUS INDUSTRIES	-	-	-	24	-	-	-	250	-	110	-	7	-	13	650	456	8	4	3	9	6	38	1	*	3
43 UNDISTRIBUTED	-	2,059	132	438	1,310	880	329	201	610	1,740	788	329	323	570	287	101	211	172	1,000	356	250	1,463	45	204	822
44 EATING & DRINKING PLACES	-	-	-	-	-	-	-	-	-	2	-	-	-	-	-	-	-	-	-	-	-	-	-	-	-
45 NEW CONSTRUCTION & MAINTENANCE	199	117	1	39	16	12	7	42	15	36	26	12	19	34	81	20	5	5	24	16	6	28	2	7	16
46 INVENTORY CHANGE (depletions)	2,660	402	1	120	185	*	14	87	26	140	8	3	33	2	3	102	-	*	3	*	*	4	-	*	2
47 FOREIGN COUNTRIES (imports from)	690	2,001	104	200	270	103	6	621	.8	594	258	2	35	143	43	573	*	1	6	35	1	16	1	1	2
48 GOVERNMENT	813	1,134	104	639	376	338	112	497	335	762	780	114	136	323	573	245	86	113	277	167	86	514	64	62	274
49 GROSS PRIVATE CAPITAL FORMATION	DEPRECIATION AND OTHER CAPITAL CONSUMPTION ALLOWANCES ARE INCLUDED IN HOUSEHOLD ROW																-	-	-	-	-	-	-	-	-
50 HOUSEHOLDS	19,166	6,262	387	3,286	4,013	2,564	1,063	2,161	3,034	3,431	4,907	1,024	1,140	2,255	3,945	1,519	624	943	2,335	1,178	930	4,339	534	595	2,092
TOTAL GROSS OUTLAYS	44,263	37,636	2,663	9,838	13,321	6,002	2,892	7,899	6,447	14,050	13,670	2,825	3,810	4,844	12,338	6,387	1,745	2,316	6,445	3,292	1,833	10,312	1,095	1,692	5,723

FINAL DEMAND (columns 46–50)

INDUSTRY PRODUCING	26 MOTOR VEHICLES	27 OTHER TRANSPORTATION EQUIPMENT	28 PROFESSIONAL & SCIENTIFIC EQUIPMENT	29 MISCELLANEOUS MANUFACTURING	30 COAL, GAS & ELECTRIC POWER	31 RAILROAD TRANSPORTATION	32 OCEAN TRANSPORTATION	33 OTHER TRANSPORTATION	34 TRADE	35 COMMUNICATIONS	36 FINANCE & INSURANCE	37 RENTAL	38 BUSINESS SERVICES	39 PERSONAL & REPAIR SERVICES	40 MEDICAL, EDUC. & NONPROFIT ORG'S	41 AMUSEMENTS	42 SCRAP & MISCELLANEOUS INDUSTRIES	43 UNDISTRIBUTED	44 EATING & DRINKING PLACES	45 NEW CONSTRUCTION & MAINTENANCE	46 INVENTORY CHANGE (additions)	47 FOREIGN COUNTRIES (exports to)	48 GOVERNMENT	49 GROSS PRIVATE CAPITAL FORMATION	50 HOUSEHOLDS	TOTAL GROSS OUTPUT
1 AGRICULTURE & FISHERIES	-	-	4	4	-	5	1	8	-	2	-	-	-	-	116	-	-	250	865	92	1,008	1,276	569	21	9,785	44,263
2 FOOD & KINDRED PRODUCTS	-	-	5	21	1	81	6	34	71	9	-	-	-	2	251	*	9	134	3,469	2	608	1,528	728	-	22,141	37,636
3 TOBACCO MANUFACTURES	-	-	-	-	*	-	-	*	-	-	-	-	-	-	-	-	7	45	-	-	77	217	3	-	1,485	2,663
4 TEXTILE MILL PRODUCTS	147	9	47	76	8	-	8	7	27	*	-	-	*	29	4	-	15	580	-	47	61	919	101	21	1,469	9,838
5 APPAREL	100	10	2	*	*	*	*	3	15	1	-	-	-	20	16	*	12	150	21	1	214	301	193	1	9,987	13,321
6 LUMBER & WOOD PRODUCTS	46	33	5	65	60	-	5	1	28	*	-	135	1	*	1	-	17	444	5	2,330	174	170	14	36	67	6,002
7 FURNITURE & FIXTURES	26	20	1	-	*	-	-	*	-	*	41	78	-	-	4	-	-	199	-	198	78	35	52	569	1,459	2,892
8 PAPER & ALLIED PRODUCTS	33	20	75	69	4	2	-	4	568	2	1	-	2	62	26	-	145	836	57	170	44	154	59	-	344	7,899
9 PRINTING & PUBLISHING	-	-	2	-	*	36	4	20	98	33	213	-	2,234	27	173	13	321	585	30	-	*	72	156	89	1,491	6,447
10 CHEMICALS	111	22	55	167	55	32	5	20	73	3	*	-	7	198	222	2	30	1,181	42	635	305	812	186	-	1,964	14,050
11 PRODUCTS OF PETROLEUM & COAL	31	11	2	8	471	270	87	448	200	2	15	780	*	57	56	1	8	357	15	617	56	680	177	*	2,437	13,670
12 RUBBER PRODUCTS	496	12	5	37	1	1	-	130	63	1	7	*	-	71	4	-	5	468	4	56	94	168	21	8	709	2,825
13 LEATHER & LEATHER PRODUCTS	13	3	8	10	*	-	-	2	2	-	-	-	-	34	6	-	14	283	-	1	108	84	30	17	2,065	3,810
14 STONE, CLAY & GLASS PRODUCTS	192	6	26	59	17	12	1	2	37	*	-	-	-	25	6	-	3	363	59	1,741	99	205	17	15	341	4,844
15 IRON & STEEL	1,102	370	16	35	44	153	-	6	-	1	-	-	-	-	-	-	130	719	-	876	57	605	13	-	-	12,338
16 NONFERROUS METALS	176	62	55	170	6	45	-	2	-	*	-	-	-	-	*	-	21	524	2	315	98	167	5	-	19	6,387
17 PLUMBING & HEATING SUPPLIES	8	6	-	-	*	-	-	-	-	-	-	-	-	-	-	-	7	106	-	878	64	42	7	60	397	1,745
18 FABRICATED STRUCTURAL METAL PRODUCTS	10	31	1	-	*	7	-	1	-	-	-	-	-	-	-	-	9	248	-	1,564	15	67	4	145	13	2,316
19 OTHER FABRICATED METAL PRODUCTS	956	62	68	38	5	26	5	7	59	1	-	-	1	32	6	-	46	1,138	24	652	127	280	38	74	537	6,445
20 AGRIC'L, MINING & CONST. MACHINERY	3	14	-	-	28	3	-	*	-	-	-	-	-	57	*	-	11	261	-	116	105	566	82	1,640	66	3,292
21 METALWORKING MACHINERY	223	12	8	*	-	8	-	1	-	-	-	-	-	-	-	-	6	264	-	-	17	205	11	734	31	1,833
22 OTHER MACHINERY (except electric)	402	195	26	3	6	47	-	12	8	-	16	-	-	146	1	-	53	1,717	-	338	288	990	84	3,450	1,080	10,312
23 MOTORS & GENERATORS	-	51	10	-	1	5	-	4	-	-	-	-	-	3	-	-	10	257	-	3	33	85	11	128	-	1,095
24 RADIOS	19	15	4	-	-	-	-	-	3	1	-	-	*	23	-	-	2	74	-	-	56	113	83	296	639	1,692
25 OTHER ELECTRICAL MACHINERY	599	53	21	18	17	30	-	8	6	49	-	-	5	62	4	-	25	608	-	716	161	244	76	1,331	673	5,723
26 MOTOR VEHICLES	4,401	*	-	-	8	*	-	131	20	*	-	*	-	1,054	*	-	70	671	1	36	401	1,020	151	2,982	3,128	14,265
27 OTHER TRANSPORTATION EQUIPMENT	12	295	-	-	*	38	76	132	-	-	-	-	-	2	-	-	14	456	-	1	18	324	1,245	1,203	171	4,001
28 PROFESSIONAL & SCIENTIFIC EQUIPMENT	70	23	176	24	*	-	-	2	-	*	-	-	7	52	176	-	6	229	-	22	32	184	79	260	630	2,119
29 MISCELLANEOUS MANUFACTURING	22	3	26	156	2	1	6	1	10	*			148	184	46	53	112	638	21	32	43	187	85	511	1,934	4,756
30 COAL, GAS & ELECTRIC POWER	62	28	10	25	1,272	443	4	91	493	10	63	3,016	5	307	163	54	-	23	219	30	27	355	195	-	133	9,205
31 RAILROAD TRANSPORTATION	228	37	14	31	151	410	3	58	75	5	6	422	27	29	52	2	10	798	253	706	74	590	332	266	2,061	9,952
32 OCEAN TRANSPORTATION	1	*	2	10	*	-	218	-	-	-	-	-	-	-	-	-	5	2	-	-	-	1,340	126	-	102	2,292
33 OTHER TRANSPORTATION	67	13	5	14	35	195	35	253	311	3	4	125	29	14	190	2	6	1,102	97	572	38	314	186	103	3,860	9,855
34 TRADE	56	74	39	48	40	30	6	423	202	7	43	747	135	386	292	7	80	808	1,061	2,506	149	987	45	2,336	27,107	41,657
35 COMMUNICATIONS	16	10	6	9	18	18	2	42	326	66	85	62	429	123	66	11	-	83	11	44	-	38	148	-	1,269	3,173
36 FINANCE & INSURANCE	22	21	6	18	48	24	120	298	1,002	5	1,851	555	22	118	93	26	-	-	72	400	-	135	32	-	6,993	12,814
37 RENTAL	21	20	11	35	46	24	7	147	1,961	52	211	208	58	710	402	180	-	-	386	84	-	-	223	804	20,289	28,855
38 BUSINESS SERVICES	76	10	51	57	9	22	2	33	1,706	86	143	37	64	121	17	95	-	421	55	134	-	3	38	-	179	5,097
39 PERSONAL & REPAIR SERVICES	3	2	1	4	16	11	5	264	1,415	16	113	25	68	559	76	22	30	2,294	228	819	-	-	83	271	7,333	14,301
40 MEDICAL, EDUC. & NONPROFIT ORG'S	-	-	-	-	-	-	*	*	-	-	16	-	-	-	85	-	-	350	-	-	-	-	5,078	-	7,856	13,385
41 AMUSEMENTS	-	-	-	-	-	-	-	-	-	-	-	-	-	-	7	392	-	14	-	-	-	128	-	-	2,403	2,944
42 SCRAP & MISCELLANEOUS INDUSTRIES	-	-	1	-	-	-	-	35	386	10	106	34	20	1	1	13	-	12	-	1	-	30	1	-	-	2,233
43 UNDISTRIBUTED	490	406	227	1,049	356	61	214	73	2,320	80	617	547	575	1,303	980	269	-	-	536	-	-	-	-	-	-	24,711
44 EATING & DRINKING PLACES	-	-	-	-	-	-	-	11	-	-	-	-	-	-	152	-	-	1,030	-	-	-	-	-	-	12,075	13,270
45 NEW CONSTRUCTION & MAINTENANCE	44	23	7	18	265	1,118	1	134	182	178	32	4,084	3	56	342	25	-	-	73	7	-	-	5,464	15,709	154	28,704
46 INVENTORY CHANGE (depletions)	7	8	47	157	*	-	-	-	-	-	-	-	-	-	-	-	851	-	-	-	-	22	-	-	-	4,887
47 FOREIGN COUNTRIES (imports from)	15	11	54	141	7	41	302	33	-	33	105	-	-	-	-	3	69	12	-	-	-	-	1,313	-	1,325	9,275
48 GOVERNMENT	656	120	134	191	1,142	1,075	256	766	3,750	344	1,111	3,997	212	503	170	318	74	2,176	1,410	470	73	831	3,458	216	31,308	63,685
49 GROSS PRIVATE CAPITAL FORMATION	-	-	-	-	-	-	-	-	-	-	-	-	-	-	-	-	-	-	-	-	-	-	-	-	-	-
50 HOUSEHOLDS	3,303	1,880	856	1,989	5,066	5,675	914	6,205	26,240	2,165	8,015	14,003	1,044	7,951	9,199	1,456	-	1,801	4,254	11,492	-	847	30,058	218	2,116	220,474
TOTAL GROSS OUTLAYS	14,265	4,001	2,119	4,756	9,205	9,952	2,292	9,855	41,657	3,173	12,814	28,855	5,097	14,301	13,385	2,944	2,233	24,711	13,270	28,704	4,802	17,320	51,060	33,514	191,625	769,248

* Less than $500,000

UNITED STATES DEPARTMENT OF LABOR
BUREAU OF LABOR STATISTICS

DIVISION OF INTERINDUSTRY ECONOMICS
OCTOBER 1951

496821 O - 59 (Face p. 4)

II
SOME COMMON ECONOMIC TERMS AND CONCEPTS

Economics, like most other subjects of instruction, has developed a number of terms and concepts with meanings peculiar to its particular body of knowledge. A short introductory discussion of some of the common economic expressions may help to prepare the student for an understanding of their later use. The cursory treatment in this chapter can be supplemented, if desired, by reference to standard full-length texts.

HUMAN WANTS

Basic economic theory is concerned with the satisfaction of human wants. Man is a complex creature with many and varying needs. As soon as the more elementary needs of food, clothing, and shelter are fulfilled, human wants turn to areas satisfied by the rendition of services by other free human beings. These service needs become more complex as leisure time, the standard of living, and the length of the life-span increase. Beyond the satisfaction of these universal needs and the service wants, man's demands are ever growing with each new acquisition. It is correct to say, then, even in a very advanced economy, that *man's wants are insatiable.* Therefore economics deals with scarcity. Almost none of us can satisfy all his wants at any given time, and we must constantly allocate our personal resources to take care of the most pressing of our current wants.

GOODS

Economic goods versus free goods. An economic good is any product or service that satisfies a human want, even though it may have moral or legal aspects frowned on by society. Such a good is said to have utility. It is usual to distinguish a free good from an economic good. A free good is one provided by nature in quantities sufficient for all. An economic good is one that requires human effort to produce. Water in a river is free good, but water piped to the kitchen sink is an economic good. Both satisfy human wants. A beautiful sunset is a free good; a painting of it is an economic good.

Consumers' goods are end products capable of directly satisfying human wants, an orange or a sweeper. *Producers' goods* or capital goods are raw materials and machines which are used in the process of further production, a sheet of steel or a lathe.

Diminishing utility. When economists speak of *diminishing utility,* they mean that successive units of the same commodity tend to yield decreasing amounts of satisfaction. Thus one ice cream soda even on a very warm day, might yield greater satisfaction and command a higher price than a second and certainly more than a fifth or sixth. This, in part, explains the fact that there is not a television set in every room.

PRODUCTION

FACTORS OF PRODUCTION

Land, labor, and *capital* are known as the *factors of production.* Each production process combines all three factors but in varying proportions. The entrepeneur, or "risk-taker", was once thought of as a part of the capital factor, since he often owned or at least controlled the capital of his firm. In another sense, he is often thought of as a special type of laborer. Today the ownership of capital of large firms is widely scattered, and many writers list entrepreneurial skill as a *fourth* factor of production. In any case the management of any firm must supply incentive and must direct and assume responsibility for the firm's business operations. The board of directors controls the capital, even though actual ownership of individual shares is scattered.

DIVISION OF LABOR

Adam Smith wrote of pinmaking and showed that pinmakers were enjoying greater production since one worker concentrated on the body of the pin, one on the point, another on the head, another dipped the pins in final tin bath, and still another packaged them. The *division of labor* simply means that each worker concentrates on the work at which he is most skillful. If all do this regularly and exchange the resulting products periodically, each must necessarily enjoy final possession of a greater variety and quality of goods than would be possible under any other system. Trade between geographical regions and between independent nations is based on this concept of the division of labor. The American mass production system carries out the division of labor to a very advanced degree. We enjoy similar specialization and subspecialization also in our learned professions.

Services. Early economists had great difficulty in satisfying themselves that certain human services were economic in nature, since no tangible product resulted from the service. They were wont to pick out the local clergyman as an example of a man performing a desired service but with no tangible product to show for his efforts. Economists today solve this problem by taking the principle of the *division of labor* as a base. The modern production process is so complicated that few workers can say they personally produce a completed product. It becomes easy then to say that all production is the result of services.

DIMINISHING RETURNS

The law of *diminishing returns* may be clarified by an example. A farmer uses a constant amount of labor and seed in cultivating a fixed amount of land, one acre. He varies the amount of fertilizer and records the effect of varying amounts. He finds that he can produce 5 bushels of wheat without any fertilizer; with one unit (25 lbs.) he produces a total of 7 bushels; with two units (50 lbs.) he produces a total of 10 bushels; and with three units (75 lbs.) he produces 12 bushels. While the second unit increased production by three bushels, the third unit resulted in an increase of only 2 bushels. The point of diminishing returns has been reached. However, the farmer would continue the application of fertilizer so long as the additional amount of wheat will sell for more than the cost of the added unit of fertilizer, that is, until he reaches the limit of profitable expansion.

The law of diminishing returns applies to industry as well as to agriculture. In any given factory or mine, with a given amount of space, and with the use of certain machinery, there is some amount of labor that will yield the greatest output per worker. Beyond that point the marginal product of labor will decline. This holds for retail stores covering a fixed amount of floor space: there is a limit to the number of clerks that can profitably be added.

The point of diminishing returns beyond which increases in labor to a fixed amount of land and capital will not yield corresponding increases of output is highly important in fixing the demand for labor and in determining its price, or wage. No entrepreneur will knowingly pay a worker more than the value of his output. Wages, therefore, cannot rise above the marginal value product of the labor, the value of output credited to the last unit of labor used. If wages are above this level, they can be paid only from profits. If workers whose wages exceed the value of their addition to output are released, the pressure of unemployment will consequently lead to a reduction in wage levels to the marginal addition to output. Wages tend to equal the marginal addition of the worker to output. Labor's share of the production income depends on the scarcity of labor relative to land and capital.

If additional amounts of *capital* are applied to fixed amounts of labor and land, with no increase in technology, a point will be reached beyond which the *marginal product of capital* will decline. Beyond the point of diminishing returns, additional supplies of capital will not yield proportional increases of output. This process helps to fix interest rates as well as land rents. The law of diminishing returns thus applies to land, labor, and capital.

RISK AND PROTECTION

Risk. Entrepreneurial effort necessarily involves risk. The degree of risk incurred varies with the stability of the enterprise.

Insurance. Although the right to any profit accruing from a business venture is the reward of the risk-taker, entrepreneurs constantly band together in attempts to insure themselves against risk. To the extent that insurance proves perfect, the right to pure profit dwindles. Insurance is a system of prorating known or anticipated risks among a group subject to those particular risks. Insurance systems are reduced to an actuarial and statistical science. It, therefore, is a known cost and is not a fortuitous gamble.

Hedging. Hedging is an insurance method employed by persons engaged in businesses that require the current delivery of commodities subject to price changes before the end product made from each commodity is ready for the market. The miller may buy wheat for immediate delivery to be processed into flour for sale four months hence. If the price of wheat and flour remains unchanged, he will realize the usual profit from milling. But prices may change, so he sells an equal amount of wheat to be delivered four months hence. If prices rise he loses on the wheat which he must buy at that date at the prevailing price but gains an equal amount on the opposing sale. Thus he is left with the anticipated profit on the flour. This speculative gain and loss exactly offset each other.

CONSUMPTION

Consumption is the end of production. It is the process of using goods and services to satisfy wants. Each individual is best able to choose the products most conducive to satisfying his desire. Consumers' desires are expressed as demands for product, coupled, of course, with the monetary means to make this demand effective. Producers respond to demand but must constantly adapt themselves to changes therein, if they are to maximize their own income.

POPULATION AS AN ECONOMIC FACTOR

Population problems have long been of interest to the economist, for there is an important relation between numbers of people, on the one hand, and both production and consumption on the other. The population has expanded over the years, but production has increased to take care of the growing demands. During the deep depression of the 1930's the rate of increase in population declined. World War II created a great demand for manpower, and the development of automation helped to overcome manpower deficiencies. During and since World War II the number of children per family has increased, and this greater number is now beginning to extend the facilities of the school and college systems. This increased supply of manpower will eventually have an impact on the labor market, the ramifications of which are not yet fully apparent.

The 18th century Malthusian theory that population tends to outrun food supply is still being discussed. Today far greater numbers than were foreseen by Malthus are being fed daily, and the standard of diet is far higher than in 1798. Barring great natural catastrophies in one or more regions of the world, there is no immediate danger that world population will exceed food supply. The long-range population problem, however, is subject to much debate.

VALUE AND PRICE

It is possible to list many kinds of *values*—moral, legal, ethical, sentimental, value-in-use, and value in the market place. Economists are called materialistic when they insist that the value of anything that *must be sold* is exactly what you can get foı it and nothing else. In any sale the price paid is the only price that could have prevailed between that particular buyer and seller at the moment of sale. If either thought he could get more or pay less, no transaction would have taken place. It is often a shock to owners, however, to find that the values placed on articles by their possessors are very different from those reflected by prices offered by others. More simply stated, the "value" of the good or service that must be sold is the quantity of other goods and services which can be obtained in exchange for it.

Price is the great common denominator of value. By putting a price on a variety of goods, we can compare them and can arrive at a single value for a mixed supply of goods. Through the price mechanism we can add the value of apples, shoes, services of a surgeon, and the enjoyment of a rendition of Brahms' Lullaby. Price also determines what goods are to be produced and how they are to be distributed.

SUPPLY AND DEMAND

In economic literature reference is frequently made to the "law" of supply and demand. It is an integral part of most economic activity and has particular applicability under a free-market system of buying and selling. Competition between buyers tends to force prices up; competition between sellers tends to force prices down. At any given moment, the market price is determined by those buyers, usually called marginal buyers, who are just willing to buy at the quoted price and by the sellers who are just willing to sell at the price offered (fig. 1).

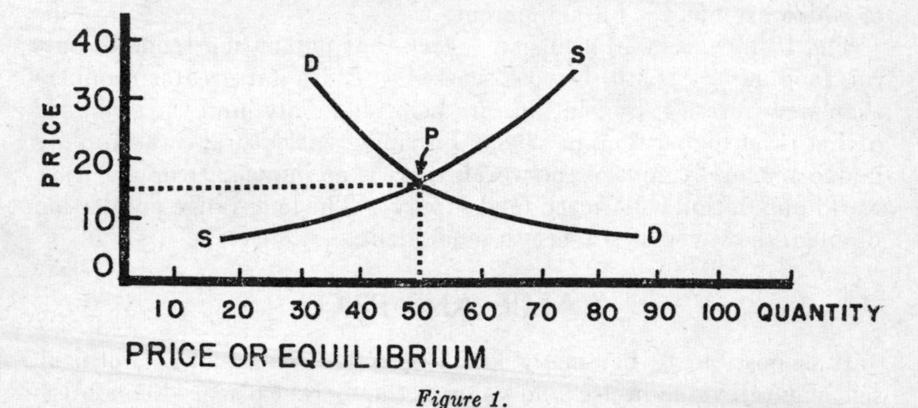

Figure 1.

In figure 1, the line SS represents the supply possibilities at the several possible prices. The line DD represents the demand (willingness to buy) possibilities at the several possible prices. The meeting point of demand and supply, point P, indicates the market price and the amount traded in that market at that time. A further analysis of demand and supply schedules follows.

DEMAND

Demand schedules. Economists like to construct demand curves or demand schedules for a product showing price in relation to quantity. A demand schedule is a table of all the amounts of a given commodity that would be bought in a given market at all possible prices. A demand curve is a graph of all prices at the amounts offered. My own demand schedule for shoes, if the price is $15 per pair, might be 1 pair. I might feel that I could afford 2 pairs at $10, 3 at $7.50, and 4 pairs at $6. My demand curve for shoes would appear as in figure 2.

If I multiply my own demand schedule by the number of persons in my community whom I estimate to have tastes and incomes similar to mine, I can estimate the total demand schedule of this group for shoes. Notice that this schedule remains an "estimate." Consider-

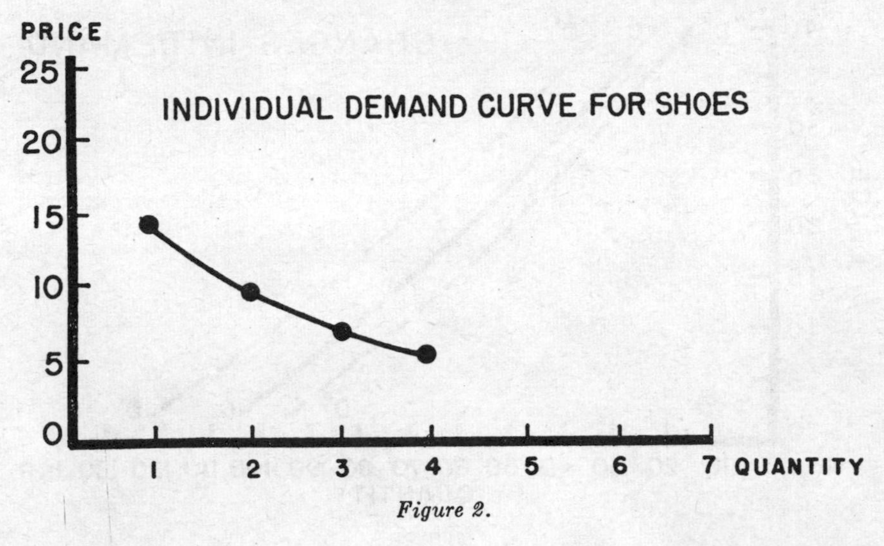

Figure 2.

able quantities of already existing goods can be disposed of readily and quickly only by lowering the price. If more units are to be sold to the same people, the price of succeeding units must be lowered, since the marginal utility of each added unit will be less to the same purchaser. If additional units are to be sold to others, they must be sold to those who were unwilling or unable to pay the previous higher price.

Changes in demand. A demand curve is thought of as existing throughout its entire length at the same time. Shift in any demand schedule can arise for any one of five reasons: (1) income changes, (2) taste changes, (3) price changes in other goods, (4) appearance of substitutes, or (5) belief by buyers that further price changes will occur. Without a change in one or more of these five conditions, the purchase of greater amounts of the same product at a lower price does not indicate a change in demand but only a *change in the quantity purchased* in response to the lower price.

The line DD in figure 3 represents a demand curve showing the amounts of some commodity that would be bought at each of several prices. The line D′D′ represents increased demand compared with that represented by DD. This means that at each of the several prices more units would be bought. The line D″D″ indicates a lessened demand.

Elasticity of demand. The demand for some goods is more elastic than that for others. The demand for bread or salt is rather inelastic. Sudden changes in price will affect demand only temporarily until other purchases can be readjusted. By and large, the same amounts will be used, day in and day out. Other demands are quite elastic

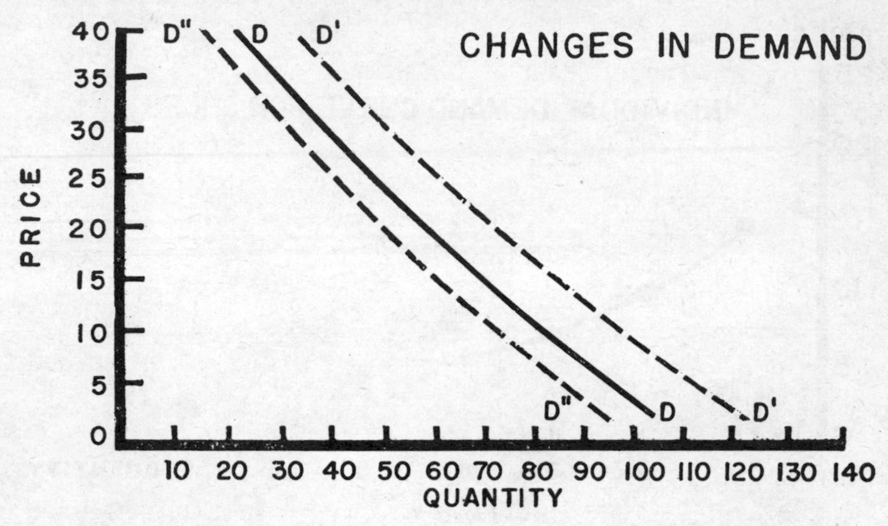

Figure 3.

and respond readily to price changes. Undoubtedly many more sport-type automobiles would be bought if the price were lowered considerably.

SUPPLY

Supply schedules. A supply schedule is a table of all amounts of goods that would be offered for sale at every possible price at any one moment. If the demand curve does not change or shift, increases or decreases in supply will result in an entirely new supply curve. If the supply increases, the supply curve moves to the right, S′S′, indicating that at the same prices represented on the former supply curve, larger quantities will be offered for sale. A supply increase means that sellers are more anxious to sell, are willing to sell more at any given price. If the supply decreases the supply curve moves to the left (fig. 4).

ECONOMIC RENT

The term economic rent is concerned with the "unearned increment." It arises in connection with land due to its fertility as a producer of food or for its location as a site for business operations or commercial farming. It is duly reflected in the contract rent charged for the use of such pieces of land.

If two pieces of land are for rent or for sale and are equal in every way except that one enjoys a ten percent differential in fertility over the other, the income to the owner should reflect this differential. The tenant or the purchaser would rather work the better land. Ricardo's statement is still worth repeating: economic rent exists

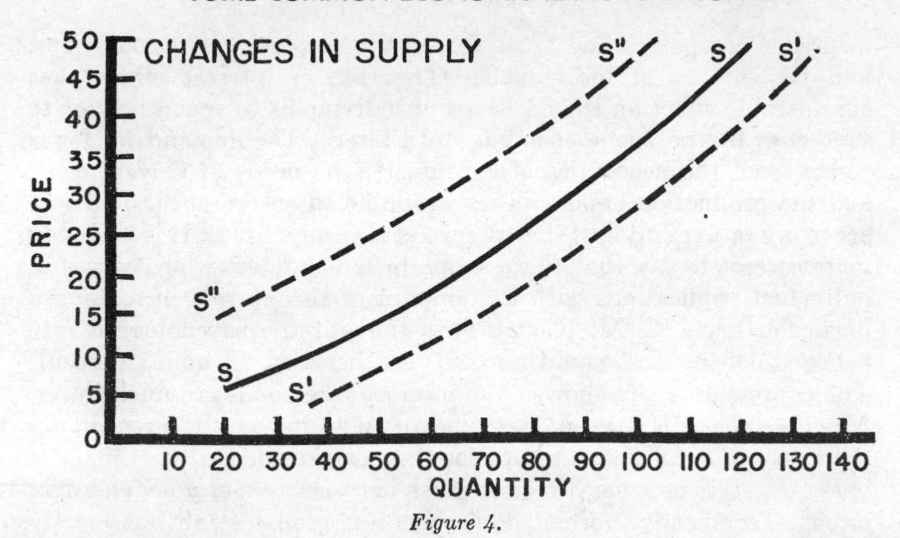

Figure 4.

because corn is high: corn is not high because economic rent exists. Poorer and poorer land must be put into cultivation until the demand for food is met. Owners of the better grades of land enjoy low costs but receive the price necessary to provide higher cost returns on the poorest land which must be used. Location-rent or site-rent is due to the location of desirable farm land near cities or to business locations within cities close to the daily paths of many people.

Utopians were not long in noting that a cow pasture that became a city lot without effort on the part of its owner nevertheless enriched him. A political group known as "single taxers" attained considerable prominence in the late 19th and early 20 centuries. They campaigned on the platform that a single, painless tax that merely absorbed the economic rent, or the unearned increment, would suffice for all urban tax revenues. Moralists feel the imposition of such a tax, at least, without a very long period of forewarning and a very gradual application, would destroy existing values and thus amount to an unwarranted and unforeseen confiscation of property. Such a system would also tend to inelasticity.

Quasi-rent is a term often applied to the use of machine tools, equipment, and plants which prove useful after their total cash have been written off through amortization or depreciation procedures.

INCOME—INTEREST, PROFIT, RENT, WAGES

Interest. Interest is the sum we must pay to use the money and capital of others. The *rate of interest* is fixed at the level which must be offered to bring out the last dollar of loans needed. The supply of loans comes from the accommodations of banks, the investments of insurance companies and trust funds, the surpluses of corporations, and the savings of individuals. The rate of interest offered has considerable effect on the decisions of individuals to spend now or to save now and postpone spending until later. The demand for loans comes from the necessities of consumers, the needs of Government, and the production opportunities available to entrepreneurs. There are many rates of interest in existence at the same time. It is probably more correct to say that there is one rate of interest which varies in individual applications with the amount of risk carried in making a particular loan. J. M. Keynes once thought the psychological rate below which interest could not fall was between 2½ and 3 percent. The depression years showed the interest rate could go much lower. *Negative interest* is a term sometimes used to indicate a payment by the owner of surpluses in return for their safekeeping.

Profit. It is necessary to distinguish between *normal profit* and *pure profit.* Technically, normal profits are not profits at all but merely payment for services performed. They consist of several items. Interest is the charge for the use of capital whether borrowed or belonging to the owners of a business. Rent is due the landlord whether or not he is also the owner of the company. Again the owner of a company should have a salary equal to that he would earn if performing the same service for another. These payments are part of the ordinary costs of doing business. *Pure profit* as such consists of any residual sums after all costs have been met. Ordinary costs, of course, include allowances for depreciation. These residual sums belong to the owners and may be used as extra dividends, bonuses, or for expansion of the firm. The mere existence of pure profit attracts newcomers to the business producing them. A firm earning normal profits has, of course, no reason to close because of the lack of pure profit, since it is earning all its costs.

Rent. The term rent as a payment for the temporary use of a durable good is sometimes called contract rent to distinguish it from economic rent. It is the amount paid to another person for the specified use of a durable good which is then to be returned to the owner.

Wages. Wages is income derived from labor—one of the factors of production. In general, wage rates are the result of supply and demand. In the modern era, however, labor organizations have considerable influence on wages through collective bargaining and a degree of control over the supply of labor. There are, of course, many factors affecting the demand for labor, such as the demand for and the price of the products of labor and the cost of producing those products compared with their price. The amount of capital investment and the amount and type of machinery used affect the demand for labor.

III

COMPETITION IN BUSINESS

DEMAND AS SEEN BY THE SELLER

The individual demand curve that faces the seller of any product depends on the type of competition existing within that particular industry. Competitive conditions in the several industries vary from pure competition to pure monopoly, with several in-between combinations.

PURE AND PERFECT COMPETITION

Pure and perfect competitive conditions require that: (1) The product must be homogeneous—one producer's product is not differentiated from that of another. (2) There must be many buyers and sellers. "Many" means enough buyers and sellers that the action of no individual buyer or seller can affect the entire market. (3) There is no restraint on either purchases or sales. (4) No supplier controls enough of the supply to affect the price by withholding and no buyer buys sufficient that his refusal to buy would affect price. (5) There is perfect knowledge of market conditions on the part of both buyers and sellers.

These conditions of competition are seldom realized in today's market place, but they are still approached in the marketing of agricultural commodities that enter world trade. Pure and perfect competition has come to be known as "textbook competition," yet most useful as a basis for discussion.

DEGREES OF MONOPOLY

Pure monopoly is a situation wherein there is no close substitute for a single firm's product. It is difficult to cite an actual example of continuing pure monopoly. Temporary monopoly based on new patents is common enough.

Public utility companies are not examples of pure monopoly since, while enjoying an exclusive franchise, they are denied the right to set their own prices. Rates are controlled by rate-limiting bodies and are based on costs of production and not on what the traffic will bear. The economist finds the concept of pure monopoly an interesting one in the abstract. What production level and what price would an intelligent monopolist select for his business? Would he limit production and deliberately seek the level at which he would enjoy the greatest profit? Or would he elect to produce a greater quantity, which would subsequently command a somewhat lower price, in order to discourage the appearance of substitutes and also to earn public goodwill? Again, under what conditions would he absorb an excise or a sales tax, and at what point would he pass it along to the consumer?

DUOPOLY

If examples of pure monopoly are hard to cite, there are many situations of semimonopoly wherein two or three producers actually do divide a market. Oftentimes such a monopoly is enjoyed due simply to the size of the firms. Firms large enough to affect the market may have grown up over long periods of time or may be the result of mergers. A new firm that would be big enough to give the older firms real competition would require a huge amount of venture capital. The Sherman Antitrust Act forbids conspiracies in restraint of trade. But we know that intelligent *duopolists* can fix prices without any conspiracy whatsoever between the two producers. One of the pair will take the action indicated by the market situation for their combined product and rely on the other to follow suit. Both must deal with unlimited competition from existing and potential substitutes for their product, but suffer only limited competition from each other.

OLIGOPOLY

Oligopoly is more frequent than duopoly. A "few" producers may be only three or just short of "many". A favorite device of oligopoly is the "suggested" price set by one producer with confidence that the others will follow suit. To the extent that he has correctly estimated the market and the conditions of production throughout the industry, the suggested price pattern will be followed. Industry trade associations contribute a great deal to make knowledge common within an industry.

IMPERFECT COMPETITION

Individual firms compete most commonly today by differentiating their products from those of their competitors to gain an edge in the struggle for favor of the consumer. Consumer psychology is most important in this form of competition. To the extent that the consumer can be convinced, perhaps through advertising, that a certain product is different from that of its competitors, the product becomes in fact different as far as that consumer is concerned. This imperfect form of competition was labeled *monopolistic competition* in 1935 by Edward Chamberlin.

Slogans are popularized by monopolistic competitors. There are many people who prefer Camel cigarettes and, it is said, "would walk a mile for a Camel." To this extent the makers enjoy a monopoly demand for their cigarettes. There are other smokers who prefer Camels as long as they do not cost more, are no more difficult to obtain, or do not require a longer walk to purchase. To this extent there is competition for their cigarette purchases. Those who would go without smoking rather than smoke another brand are bound to one producer as successfully as if he were a pure monopolist. But the producer must deal with his competitors for the business of those who merely prefer his product as long as it costs no more.

This type of imperfect or monopolistic competition is most common throughout the western world and certainly is usual in the United States. Even though we do not enjoy pure and perfect competitive conditions, which are said to be best for the consumer strictly from a price standpoint, we do have very real competition in the majority of businesses today. There is very real competition in price, in quality, in services rendered, in advertising, and in salesmanship.

The economist must never forget the "principle of substitution" in his analysis of businessmen's competition for the patronage of the consumer. Even a monopolist must face competition from substitute products and from substitute methods as well. Quilted cotton is a warm clothing fabric in lieu of wool, to cite a single example.

EQUILIBRIUM

All of us desire that our lives and living conditions shall be in some sort of rough equilibrium. Businessmen are no exception. If left to themselves, they will adjust output to the level at which their total revenues will exceed their total costs by the greatest amount. When a single firm has reached this ideal situation, it has "maximized its gains." But no single firm can be in equilibrium long if the whole industry is not enjoying this ideal condition. If it is not too difficult for new firms to enter an industry, any unusual rate of profit will attract newcomers to that industry. Within an industry itself, an old firm may enlarge its plant to gain efficiency or to install better machinery for the same purpose. It must then find a market for the greater amount of resulting product. If it cuts prices or increases discounts, it may well upset the entire industry and cause a whole new alignment between producers and purchasers.

An entire industry will be in equilibrium only when there is no motive for the number of individual firms within the industry to be increased or decreased and when there is no motive for those firms already in the industry either to expand production or to contract it.

Let the reader's own imagination suggest the time and conditions under which such an equilibrium would be possible. There are many other factors which could be cited as disturbing influences to any possible equilibrium—changes in demand for the raw materials basic to an industry, new inventions, changes in tastes, improvements in manufacturing efficiency, mergers and amalgamations, to say nothing of recession and depression.

Changes in tastes, new products, substitutes for old ones, new inventions, new manufacturing methods, and new selling methods are occurring at all times. Any of these occurrences tends to upset existing equilibriums. In order to purchase an entirely new product, many consumers will have to give up their previous demand for other products. Thus an old industry can be upset by the appearance of a new product with which it is neither in direct competition nor for which it is even substitutable. Such events are beyond the control of existing firms and industries.

PROTECTIVE PRACTICES

Business firms individually do what they can to protect themselves. They cover risks by insurance to the extent possible. Physical risks from fire and flood are covered by insurance pools. There are other agreements possible within an industry which will give some measure of insurance from risk. These include common pricing practices, sometimes called *administered prices*, the division of territory, either to produce exclusively or to sell exclusively therein, or a set of manufacturing or sales practices common to the entire industry.

As stated, conspiracy to fix prices is forbidden in the United States, as is any favoring of individual customers through larger discounts. Cartels are often legal and cartel practices are common throughout Europe and in England. It may be argued that cartel practices do bring about some degree of stabilization within an industry and thus stabilize employment. On the other hand, they institutionalize practices, inhibit dynamic growth, stratify wages, and keep prices up to the cost level required by the least efficient plant allowed to remain within the cartel.

LARGE AND SMALL FIRMS

In the United States we find many small companies existing alongside giants in the same business. The small companies could not hope to win in price competition. But they serve the purposes of the giants by handling small orders and orders requiring special formulas or special sizes. There is all-around happiness within the industry, a sort of *industrial symbiosis*.

The chain store revolutionized the retail grocery business in the 1920's, and the discount house is accomplishing the same result in wholesaling and retailing of consumer durables in the 1950's. Large consolidations have taken place in the steel, chemical, automobile, and rubber industries, and the appearance of new firms in any of these fields is now most difficult. On the other hand, no such consolidations have occurred in the textile, clothing, shoes, machinery, and construction industries.

AGRICULTURAL PARITY PRICING

Following World War I, agricultural prices slumped from their wartime levels and failed to recover. The prices of manufactured products decreased somewhat from their war levels, but the disparity between prices received by farmers and prices paid by farmers continued until the crash of 1929. Depending on one's definition for rural living, between one-quarter and one-third of the people of the United States were living on the land in the "'tween wars" period. One of the explanations for the crash of 1929 is this continuing disparity between standards of living for rural and urban groups. The 1929 program of financial aid to farmers was intensified in 1933 and included the principle of *parity pricing.* Parity was defined as that level of prices of basic farm commodities that would give the farmer's dollar the same purchasing power in nonfarm products as it had on the average during the years 1909–14. Since 1933 farm prices have been constantly supported under various types of legislation at varying parities, sometimes as high as 110 percent. In 1954 Congress reduced these support prices somewhat. There has been much postwar discussion as to whether or not the parity system is sound. The problem is complicated by the mechanization of farms and farming during World War II, which greatly increased potential production and reduced the percentage of the population living on the land. In 1956 a "soil-bank" program was set up allowing payments to farmers for taking certain lands out of cultivation.

REGULATION OF PUBLIC UTILITIES[1]

Public utilities that are Government-owned are usually known as public industries. Those privately owned are subject to Government regulation and to control of rates and earnings. Such publicly regulated industries usually include the railroad, electric, gas, water, telephone, telegraph, street railway, air transport, motor transport, some pipeline, and express companies. Industries regulated as public

[1] Public utilities and services is discussed in volume IX, *Transportation*. The electric, gas, and telecommunications industries are treated in volume X.

utilities have certain definite characteristics. They tend toward monopoly due to high fixed investments and decreasing costs. The large amount of capital needed tends to eliminate competition as an effective means of regulation. The duplication of services, such as two city transportation systems, would be prohibitively costly. Accordingly, in order to maintain regular rates and services, there are many fields of public utilities in which the local governmental authority will not permit the entrance of competing companies. Industries regulated as public utilities are said to affect vitally the public welfare.

The degree of regulation over the industries mentioned and, hence, the amount of direct competition prevailing vary from extensive control of railroads to limited control of pipelines. Originally the regulation of these industries was achieved by competition or by State laws. Indirect competition or competition between similar services is still important. For example, railroads compete with motor carriers for both freight and passenger traffic; a city transportation system competes with taxis and private cars; and electricity competes with other methods of heating and lighting.

One of the most controversial types of regulation that applies to many utilities is the fixing of rates. Rates may be based on the value of service principle, on the cost of service principle, or on a fair return on a fair evaluation. But what is a fair evaluation? Should the rate base be determined by the reproduction cost method or by the original cost method? Opinions on this score are many and varied. This is a matter of importance to the public, since the higher the rate base, the higher the justifiable rates.

COMBINATIONS IN RESTRAINT OF TRADE

The common law forbade undue restraint of trade, but it was not until 1890 that the Sherman Antitrust Act became Federal law. It declares, "Every contract, combination in the form of trust or otherwise, or conspiracy, in restraint of trade or commerce among the several states, or with foreign nations, is hereby declared to be illegal." In 1911 the Supreme Court held the Act means to prohibit not all combinations in restraint of trade, but only those which unreasonably restrain trade. This "rule of reason" regarding combinations reestablished the older common-law distinction between reasonable and unreasonable restraint of trade. Since that date the Sherman Antitrust Act has served the country well. Many additional acts have come into existence designed to solve particular problems, but the original comprehensive act stays in the statutes and is available to the Department of Justice for use in new situations, which constantly seem to crop up.

The Clayton Antitrust Act of 1914 is an omnibus measure, the main trend of which is to prevent control by combination of a part of any industry large enough to lessen competition or to tend to create monopoly. The Federal Trade Commission Act, also of 1914, sets up a Commission whose function is to prevent unfair methods of competition in commerce. Here again the powers are broad and have had many uses. The Commission need not wait for the occurrence of some overt wrong but can act in advance by helping to build up high standards of competition. It has far-reaching powers of investigation. The Robinson-Patman Act of 1936 is an amendment to the Clayton Act. The emphasis in this Act is upon practices that are destructive of competition. Persons engaged in interstate commerce may not grant or receive, directly or indirectly, any discriminations in price or service in the sale of commodities when such discrimination substantially lessens competition. The Act applies to competition among manufacturers, wholesalers, or certain classes of retailers. Price differences based on cost differences are possible, but there must be no discriminations. The Federal Trade Commission is authorized to set limits on quantity sales discounts to prevent quantity purchases at lower prices from tending to destroy competition.

The discussion of governmental policies regarding public utilities and combinations in restraint of trade points out that Government control is designed in some cases to eliminate competition, in others to maintain competition, and in still others to assure fair competition.

IV
MONEY AND THE MONETARY SYSTEM

In the history of mankind many things have been used for money, from seashells to immovable pieces of stone. The precious metals, however, have enjoyed the greatest popularity for use as money. The chief characteristic of any form of money is that it be *generally acceptable.*

FUNCTIONS AND QUALITIES OF MONEY

The four functions of money are as follows: (1) as a medium of exchange, (2) as a standard of value, (3) as a standard of deferred payment, and (4) as a store of value. Some writers assign money a fifth function, as a "reserve" that may be used to support bank deposits and note circulation.

As a *medium of exchange* money expedites the transfer of commodities from hand to hand, thus avoiding the more cumbersome barter. It also serves as a means of payment for services rendered by free people. As a *standard of value* money acts as a common denominator by which the values of a mixed group of articles can be added through means of their prices. The value of one article may be compared with that of an entirely different type by mentioning the price of each. The function of money as a standard of value is closely linked to its function as a *standard of deferred payment,* which permits a definite understanding of the conditions under which a debt is to be repaid sometime in the future. As a *store of value* an individual is able to store purchasing power for the future by simply holding money.

The qualities of money are listed under six headings: (1) General acceptability is a characteristic without which money cannot circulate. (2) Relative stability of value in the past was gained by use of the precious metals but currently is maintained through control by central banks. (3) Durability was achieved through metal coins. (4) Portability is a quality that requires high value in small bulk. It is achieved by the precious metals and through the use of credit money. (5) Divisibility can be achieved by both small coins and notes of different values. Originally this quality related to the metals since a fourth of an ounce had exactly one-fourth the value of an ounce. This was not true of certain commodities, a bear skin for example. (6) Cognizability was once attained mainly through coins, but today traveler's checks are also easily recognized.

Today we use credit money, consisting of checks and drafts, and large amounts of paper money. We carry Government printed notes instead of the more bulky bullion and write checks on deposit accounts. We depend on the Government to issue the notes and to supervise the banks, which achieves both acceptability and reliability.

While gold and silver no longer circulate freely, confidence is still closely attached to the "hard" currencies. There is a psychological tieup between the knowledge of the existence of precious metals somewhere in the monetary system of a country and confidence in that system (fig. 5).

KINDS OF MONEY

Standard money. The technical term *standard money* describes the unit of a nation's currency by which all others are measured. In the United States it is the dollar, that is, the "gold dollar." Today the American dollar has a gold base but is not fully backed by gold. It must be backed by at least 25 percent gold, according to statute, but is actually backed by more than 40 percent gold. Even though our paper money cannot now be freely converted into gold, the Gold Standard Act of 1900 requires the Secretary of the Treasury to keep all forms of United States money on a par with gold. All forms of United States currency and coins are full legal tender and must be accepted in payment of debt.

Fiduciary money. Money without full intrinsic value but which is accepted in the belief that others will readily take it at face value is known as *fiduciary money.* Most subsidiary coins which have a coin value greater than their metal value and all paper money are really fiduciary in type. They are of importance only in domestic commerce, since gold bullion is still the language of international trade.

Gold-standard monetary systems. In theory, a gold standard, either coin or specie, stabilizes both the domestic price level and the foreign exchange rate of a nation. Under a free gold standard, one may exchange all forms of money for gold coins at will, may possess specie, or may have it coined freely at the mint. This free gold standard exists almost nowhere today.

Currently the world is using several lesser gold standards. A *gold bullion standard* allows the withdrawal of gold bars from the Government storehouse when they are to be used in the industrial arts or to settle international trade balances. The gold, however, cannot be coined under such a standard.

At times a nation may use a *gold-exchange standard* to settle its international trade balances. A country not on the gold standard itself may keep a supply of gold in another hard-currency country against which bills of exchange may be drawn. The gold-exchange standard

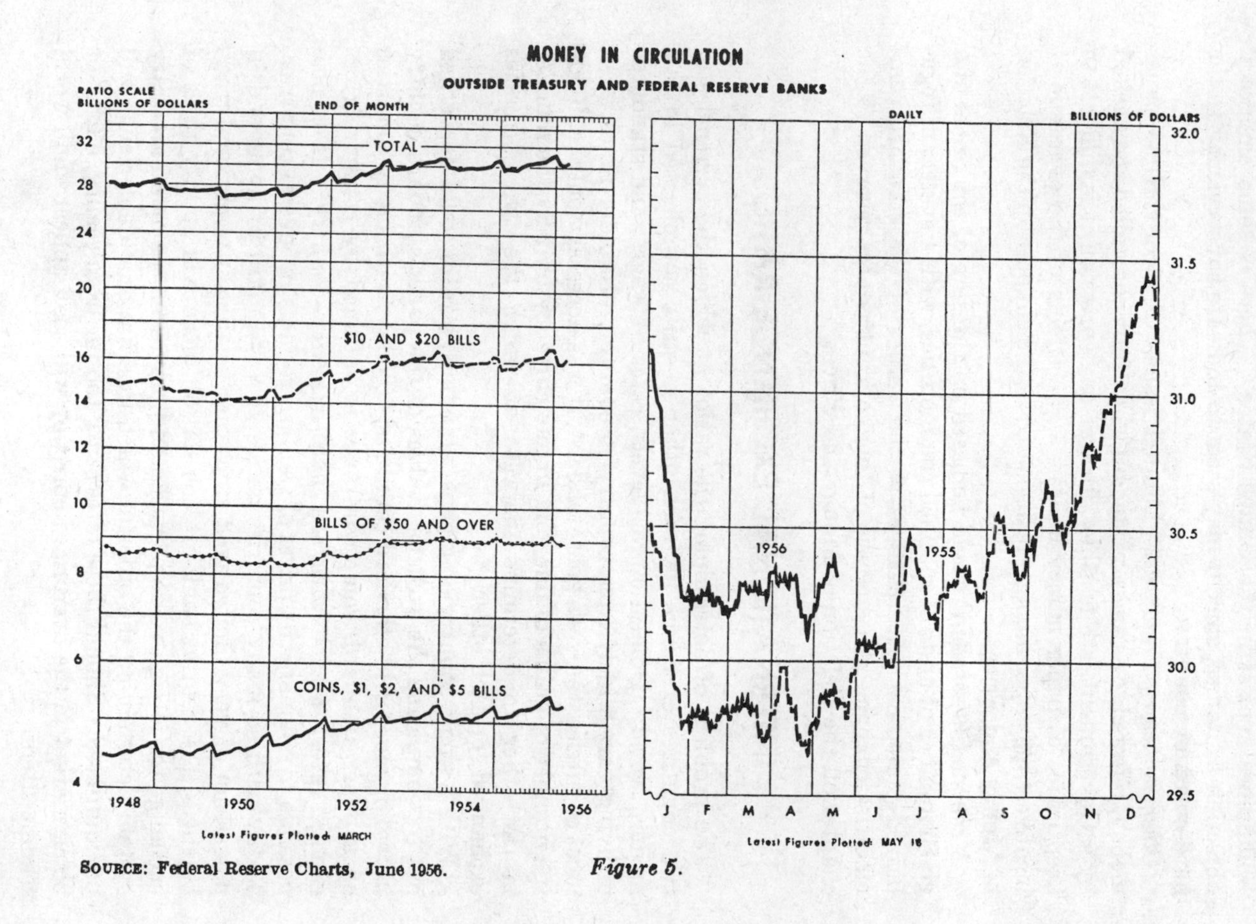

SOURCE: Federal Reserve Charts, June 1956.

Figure 5.

requires less gold than a free gold standard. It was often used by countries on a silver standard. India kept gold in England; the Philippines kept it in the United States. There is some emotional objection to its use, since it may seem to indicate subserviency to the hard-currency country.

Other monetary standards. Limited issues of inconvertible paper money, referred to as a *paper standard* when fully controlled and backed by a Government, are feasible. In war or depression it is difficult to keep issues of paper money limited. The effects of the overissue of inconvertible paper money are discussed in the chapter on the Relation of Money and Prices.

A *commodity standard* would be based on the sum of the prices of a given number of units of specified commodities, with a system of regularized periodical price changes as the values of the standard commodities change. An analysis of this concept is also reserved to the chapter on the Relation of Money and Prices.

INTERNATIONAL EXCHANGE RATIOS

The problem of determining the ratios at which the currencies of two countries exchange for each other is quite complicated in this modern world. Domestic price levels, rates of wages, and standards of living vary widely from country to country. In older times when most countries were on a gold standard, it was necessary only to divide the number of grains of fine gold in one currency unit by the number in the other to determine the rate at which the two currencies exchanged for each other.

With a single country on a paper standard, a ratio could be worked out by comparing the exchange values of the paper-standard country in two or more gold-standard countries. Today, with many countries on a paper standard, some assistance is obtained by comparing exchange rates of each with any hard-currency country. It is also possible to compare the prices of similar products in several countries. Today with so many countries on a paper standard at home and in possession of very limited gold stocks for settling international trade balances, the central bank of each nation often will specify rates of exchange for foreign-trade purposes and may even set up an arbitrary system determining the order in which international debt claims will be liquidated. Should these rates stray too far from reailty, a gray or black market in the overpriced currency will soon appear in all world trade centers.

GRESHAM'S LAW

The monetary law which bears the name of Queen Elizabeth's mint master, Sir Thomas Gresham, was known and respected many years before he formalized it. "When two monies of unequal value are in circulation, the bad money tends to drive out the good." Gresham's law in the strict sense applies to coins only, but some of its philosophy underlies modern credit transactions; certainly no one challenges the underlying principle.

In previous times various governments designated both gold and silver as standard money, specifying definite ratios of exchange between the two metals. Both gold and silver are commodities, are used extensively in the industrial arts, and have a free-market value apart from their value as money. If either tends to become overvalued as a commodity in the market place, only the overvalued metal will circulate as money and the undervalued one will be hoarded. Many systems of bimetallism have been tried in the past, and many more have been seriously proposed. Some systems fixed definite ratios, and some provided a system of rapid ratio changes; none is important today.

THE MONETARY SYSTEM OF THE UNITED STATES

All forms of money in the United States since 1933 are legal tender in any amounts. Prior to that time some forms of paper money were only warehouse receipts for gold and silver while others were merely promises to pay issued by commercial banks.

All gold and gold certificates were called in by the Treasury during the "bank holiday" of 1933. Federal Reserve Banks are now permitted to hold gold certificates as evidence of the "ownership" of gold stored and controlled by the Government. Gold may be withdrawn only in limited amounts for use in the industrial arts and for the payment of international debts.

Silver certificates issued against silver held by the Treasury and Federal Reserve notes based on gold circulate freely. Our subsidiary coins are very much overvalued as to metal content.

The United States is not on an orthodox gold standard, nor is it on a managed paper standard. Domestically we have an inconvertible paper money managed by the Federal Reserve System but not divorced entirely from gold. International balances are paid in gold bullion. There is no single "label" by which it can be described, but the system is operating well.

V

BANKS AND THE BANKING SYSTEM

THE CREDIT SYSTEM OF EXCHANGE

Credit transactions in the United States take several forms. (1) Most raw materials and the semiprocessed goods used in manufacturing, practically all goods sold at wholesale, and a great deal of those sold at retail, are shipped "on order," with a demand for payment following at a later date. This kind of credit is granted merely to facilitate the process of exchange. (2) Of more importance as credit instruments are the "promissory notes" given to commercial banks by manufacturers, wholesalers, and retailers. The proceeds of these loans are really working capital to the borrower. The goods are made and sold during the average 90-day period of the loan, which can then be repaid, while another amount is often borrowed simultaneously to finance a new group of transactions. (3) Consumers borrow money to finance the purchase of consumer durables such as refrigerators, stoves, dishwashers, washing machines, and automobiles. Consumer loans for a period of 6 to 24 months must be repaid in monthly installments. Consumer credit may take the form of loans from banks, but is more likely to come from various types of private credit corporations. The loan corporations pay the seller *in toto* and collect monthly from the buyer, at a fee of course. (4) Investment credit takes the form of long-term loans invested in the fixed assets of a business. Only a small portion can come, under law, from the commercial banks. Mortgage bonds are issued by a company needing money and are sold to investors through investment firms organized for this purpose.

Promissory notes. A promissory note is a debtor's promise to pay. The loan obtained from the note may be secured by the deposit of collateral, usually in the form of stocks and bonds, or it may be unsecured, based on the individual's or the individual firm's reputation and background.

Checks. Checks are really forms of the sight draft. They constitute an order on a bank by a depositor to pay a third party or himself. They are ordinarily used to settle only one transaction and are the equivalent of cash.

Drafts. A draft is an order to pay issued by a creditor and directed to a debtor, often through the offices of a third party such as a bank. It may be payable at sight or at some specified future date. A draft becomes an "acceptance" when the debtor writes "accepted" across the face of the draft and signs his name. Drafts accepted by an individual are known as *individual acceptances*, those accepted by a firm are *commercial acceptances*, and those accepted by banks are *banker's acceptances*. Banker's acceptances are common in international trade. The bank accepts the draft but only after prior arrangements with the individual who is to receive the goods covered by the draft. Domestic acceptances have not proved popular in the United States. They are little used except as a means of coercing a tardy debtor.

TYPES OF BANKS

A *commercial bank* is a corporation organized for profit and operated under some degree of control by State or Federal authorities. Commercial banks accept funds for deposits which they use, in part, to supply industry with circulating capital as short-term, self-liquidating loans. Today every bank strives to meet competition from all other types of banks. It has come to resemble a department store in the variety of its functions and may include a trust department, a savings department, an investment department, and a foreign exchange department. It may also operate safe-deposit vaults.

Commercial banks handle demand deposits, and checks drawn against these deposits are our chief means of financial payment. Such checks are often known as "checking-account money." Savings, usually in rather small installments or amounts, are accepted by *savings banks* as deposits to be invested as securely as possible at definite but moderate rates of interest. Institutions which administer estates and trusts are usually known as *loan and trust companies*. They carry out financial missions for their customers but are limited by law as to the types of investment they may make. They are also likely to have permission to accept demand deposits. Investment firms are sometimes called *investment banking houses* and are often organized as individual proprietorships or partnerships. They underwrite corporate securities and also finance international transfers.

Special mortgage banks. Federal Land Banks finance agricultural financial needs covering real estate, livestock, and warehouse products. Federal Home Loan Banks operate largely through building and loan associations to finance the purchase of homes. The Reconstruction Finance Corporation, now largely liquidated, made loans to banks to liquidate frozen credits and to strengthen their structures. It also lent money to railroads, insurance companies, and industrial corporations.

Other credit institutions. Note brokers, commercial paper houses, building and loan associations, and various types of small loan institutions carry on finance and credit operations. They are not classified as banks.

FUNCTIONS OF COMMERCIAL BANKS

Commercial banks, as has been pointed out, receive demand deposits subject to withdrawal by check. No interest may be paid on such deposits in the United States. They also accept *time deposits* for definite periods of time and at interest. Bank deposits arise from: (a) funds derived from the income of the depositor, (b) the proceeds of drafts left for collection, (c) loans obtained from the bank itself, and (d) from the purchase by the banking system of other assets from nonbank holders.

The function of *clearing* among commercial banks is a very important one. Checks of one customer drawn on another customer of the same bank merely require a bookkeeping operation on the part of the bank to clear them. As between banks, however, the operation is more complicated. All of the banks within a city send messengers to a central place once or twice each day, to clear checks drawn on each other. The daily operations of clearing houses largely cancel out, one bank owing the others about the same sum as is due from them. Accumulated differences are paid by deficit banks at frequent intervals. New York and Philadelphia banks clear once an hour. The twelve Federal Reserve Banks clear by wire daily.

To make loans to depositors, short-term loans, which serve as working capital to businessmen, is the chief function of commercial banks. These loans may be made at interest or at discount. If at interest, the interest charge is merely added to the face of the loan; if at discount, the interest is deducted from the face of the loan at the time of its approval the proceeds being left for deposit.

Loans to depositors may be collateral loans but are more likely to be unsecured loans, granted on the general credit standing and background of the individual businessman or firm. Nonpayment of the latter results only in a general claim on the assets of the borrower. A current profit-and-loss statement of each individual business borrower is kept in the bank files and replaced at intervals. Loans to business borrowers are usually for ninety days, subject to renewal under conditions set by the bank. An active business has a definite "line of credit" authorized at all times. Banks require complete liquidation of loans by each borrower from time to time, at least once during each year.

THE FEDERAL RESERVE SYSTEM

The United States does not have a central bank as do most European countries. Central banks often control note issues and always carry out government policy. Under the Federal Reserve Act of 1913, the United States may be said to have a "centralized" banking system. There are twelve Federal Reserve Banks, each located in a commercial region or agricultural area. Each of the twelve is "owned" by its member banks. Each member bank buys stock in its Federal Reserve Bank in the amount of 6 percent of its paid-up capital and surplus but only half of this amount has been called in. Mutual savings banks buy stock to the extent of 1 percent of their liabilities.

The member banks of each of the Federal Reserve Banks are the national banks and such other qualified banks within that district as wish to join the Federal Reserve System. The national banks existing at the time the Federal Reserve System was formed had been chartered under the National Banking Act of 1863. They enjoyed a note-issue privilege based on the ownership of specified Government bonds. This privilege passed to the Federal Reserve System in 1914.

Member bank reserves. Each member bank is required to keep reserves with the Federal Reserve Bank of its district equal to a certain percentage of its deposits. Member banks in the "Central Reserve Cities," New York and Chicago, maintain a minimum of 13 percent of their demand deposits with their Federal Reserve Bank. The Board of Governors of the Federal Reserve System may, by law, increase this sum up to 26 percent of deposits, as required by current business conditions. Member banks in 52 other large cities, known as "Reserve Cities," maintain a minimum reserve of 10 percent of their deposits with the Reserve Bank. "Country banks" maintain 7 percent of their deposits as reserves. The reserve percentages of both the Reserve cities and the country banks may be increased up to twice the above amounts by the Board of Governors. The reserve requirement against time deposits is 3 percent subject to the authority of the Board of Governors to double this amount; the present requirement is 5 percent.

District Federal Reserve Bank reserves. The twelve Federal Reserve Banks must themselves maintain a reserve against the deposits of their member banks and also against the notes which each has outstanding. The reserves must be at least 25 percent in gold, represented by gold certificates received for their gold deposited with the Treasury. In 1955 this gold actually constituted a reserve of 47 percent behind the Federal Reserve notes outstanding. The same gold may be counted against both deposits (reserves) and notes (collateral). The balance must be made up by the note obligations of business or by Government bonds.

Federal Reserve notes. Prior to 1914 the currency of the United States consisted principally of Treasury notes secured by both gold and silver and of National Bank notes secured by specified kinds of United States Government obligations. The obligations against which notes could be issued were rather limited and the currency was extremely inelastic.

Since 1914 the amount of currency in existence expands and contracts in accordance with the needs of the public. Federal Reserve notes, which are now the principal form of currency, are paid out by a Federal Reserve Bank to its member banks as requested. The amount is charged to the member's reserve account. In turn the Federal Reserve Bank obtains the notes themselves from its Federal Reserve Agent, a representative of the Government.

The Federal Reserve Bank must pledge to its Federal Reserve Agent collateral consisting of gold certificates, Government securities, or discounted short-term businessmen's paper, at least equal to the amount of the notes issued. As currency is returned to the banks, the collateral is redeemed. Thus the banking system always has as much or as little currency as it has business transactions. Federal Reserve notes constitute about seven-eighths of all the currency now in circulation. All other American currency is Treasury currency. It includes United States notes, remnants of Civil War financing, various issues of paper money in the process of retirement, silver certificates issued against deposits of silver, silver coins, nickels, and cents.

Powers of Federal Reserve System. Although the Federal Reserve Banks "belong" to their members, control is exercised by the Board of Governors of the Federal Reserve System sitting in Washington. The Board is appointed by the President and is an independent Government agency. However, the board of directors of member banks exercises the normal management functions of private corporations.

The Board of Governors has certain specified powers of control, three of which are of paramount importance: (1) It may increase, up to doubling, the basic reserve requirements of the member banks. In this way it encourages or discourages banks in their loan policies. (2) It supervises the discount rates of the twelve Federal Reserve Banks. Any bank may take the promissory notes of businessmen to its Federal Reserve Bank and borrow on them at an announced rate of interest or discount. Today banks usually borrow on their stock of Government bonds. Of course these banks are examined periodically. However, the raising or lowering of the discount rate is an indication to the banks of the thinking of the District Federal Reserve Bank and the Board of Governors as to whether general business conditions indicate a tightening or loosening of commercial loans. While the effect of raising or lowering the discount rate is now largely psychological, the cost effect is a factor also, and the Board's action furnishes guidance to the member banks. (3) Through the open market operations of the Federal Open Market Committee, the Federal Reserve System can actually increase or decrease the deposits of member banks. If the Committee sells bonds in the open market, the process causes buyers of the bonds to draw checks in payment, thus lowering the deposit levels of the individual banks. The Committee may buy bonds as well, turning over Federal Reserve Bank funds in payment. The sellers of the bonds receive payment therefor and naturally deposit these funds, increasing the deposit holdings of the individual banks. Many are puzzled as to what causes individuals to buy or sell as the Committee moves into or out of the market place. The answer is simple: offers to buy or to sell are made attractive enough to promise a profit to the individual concerned.

If the deposits of individual banks increase, it becomes possible for them to make additional loans, or at least to refrain from "calling" loans already outstanding. If deposits decrease, the individual banks can make no further loans and may have to refuse renewals on outstanding loans as they become due.

FEDERAL DEPOSIT INSURANCE CORPORATION

The Federal Deposit Insurance Corporation operates under the Banking Acts of 1933 and 1935. The insurance of deposits was made mandatory for members of the Federal Reserve System and optional for others. Insured banks pay an annual assessment of 0.085 percent of their average deposit liabilities as an insurance premium. Deposits of each person are now insured up to $10,000. The same individual may have fully insured accounts in different banks. The Federal Deposit Insurance Corporation acts as receiver for unsound banks. Building and loan associations have a similar but separate insurance system.

HOW THE BANKING SYSTEM WORKS

Assume that there is only one commercial bank in the United States, that it is the sole member bank in the Federal Reserve System, and that all the people keep their demand deposits with this bank and obtain all loans therefrom. Assume that the member bank has enough resources to represent all the banks in the country. (These assumptions are for illustration only, and the fact that they are not correct will very much affect our later conclusions.) Assume that the relevant items in its balance sheet are as follows (in billions of dollars):

Loans and investments	80
Reserves with the Federal Reserve	20
Demand deposits	100

(Ratio of reserves to demand deposits, 20 percent.)

If it is assumed that this 20 percent ratio of reserves to demand deposits is the legal minimum, the bank would not be in a position to make any additional loans or investments. Its funds would be in use up to the limit permitted by law. Assume further that the Federal Reserve believes additional loans are desirable and that its actions add $10 billion to the member bank's reserves in a manner that also increases the bank's demand deposits by the same amount, then the simplified balance sheet of the bank would be:

Loans and investments	80
Reserves	30
Demand deposits	110

(Ratio of reserves to demand deposits, 27.3 percent.)

The member bank would have a higher ratio of reserves to deposits, 27.3 percent, than is required by law, 20 percent. Therefore, it could make additional loans and investments. The bank has the $22 billion of reserves required for its deposits of $110 billion, and also has $8 billion of excess reserves.

If it is assumed that the public is eager to borrow as much as the member bank will lend and that the proceeds of the loans will be kept on deposit with the bank, the member bank can add $40 billion to its loans and investments on the basis of the $8 billion of excess reserves. The bank's balance sheet would then be:

Loans and investments	120
Reserves	30
Demand deposits	150

(Ratio of reserves to demand deposits, 20 percent.)

Reserve banking action can provide the basis for an increase in the money supply not merely by the amount that it adds to the bank's reserves but by about five times that amount. Suppose the Federal Reserve action reduces the $20 billion of reserves the member bank had in the first place by $5 billion, at the same time lowering deposits by an equal amount. The ratio of reserves to demand deposits would be only 15.8 percent and the bank would have to call loans or sell investments to raise its deficient reserves by $4 billion, and thus absorb deposits to the extent of five times its deficiency in reserves, that is, by $20 billion.

Although the above picture of bank transactions is much over simplified, this calculation shows what a powerful instrument reserve banking action can be. Our consolidated bank can expand its loans and investments by as much as $40 billion if Federal Reserve action adds $10 billion to its reserves. No individual bank can do that because borrowers may wish to take the money out of the lending bank and they will probably write checks which may also lead to withdrawals of cash. Since the banker cannot assume that the funds thus paid out will return in the form of deposits in his bank, he does not lend more than he has in reserve funds in excess of requirements. If he did, he might not be able to honor the checks of his other depositors.

How then can the banking system, all banks together, lend about four times as much as is obtained from the Federal Reserve? When a member bank receives a deposit of $100 in currency or in the form of a check on another bank, it must, holding to the earlier assumption of a 20 percent reserve requirement, deposit $20 with a Reserve Bank as required reserves. It is free to lend or invest the remaining $80. (Actually it will keep a little of the $80 since it will need some ready till cash to meet demands of depositors.) The remaining $80 can be lent and paid out at once by the borrower to someone who deposits it at another bank. The second bank holds $16 as reserve against the new deposit of $80 and can lend the remaining $64. This sequence can be traced through many banks until $500 of demand deposits have grown out of the original $100 deposit.

It is not correct to say that, since the banking system can lend several times as much as its reserves, individual banks create money by a stroke of the pen. An individual bank can lend or invest only on the basis of money provided by its stockholders, its depositors, or its borrowing, and the maximum it can lend or invest is the excess over what it must hold as reserves. Only the Federal Reserve has the power to create or extinguish the money which serves as the reserves of banks. New reserve money, after it leaves the hands of the first bank acquiring it, continues to expand into deposit money as it passes from bank to bank, until deposits stand in some established multiple relation to the additional reserve funds.

Three additional points about the functioning of the banking system are worth noting at this stage: (1) Bank credit and monetary expansion on the basis of newly acquired reserves takes place only through a series of transactions. This takes time and thus delays the multiplying effect of new bank reserves. (2) For expansion to take place at all, there must be a demand for bank credit by credit-worthy borrowers, those whose financial standing is such as to entail a likelihood the loan will be repaid at maturity and/or an available supply of low-risk investment securities such as would be appropriate for banks to purchase. (3) The reserve banking power to create or extinguish high-powered money is exercised through a specific market mechanism. The initiative may be assumed by the Federal Reserve, or it may be taken by the member banks through borrowing or repayment of borrowing at the Federal Reserve. Thus Federal Reserve action can bring about large changes in the flow of credit and money by undertaking relatively small operations.

VI
THE RELATION OF MONEY AND PRICES

Money changes in value due to the interplay of the supply of and demand for money. These changes in the value of money are registered as changes in the "general level of prices." The value of money, the general price level, represents the ratio at which money is exchanged for goods. Changes in the general price level reflect changes either in the price paid for the commodity used as money or in the relation of the amount of money in existence to the supply of goods and services available for purchase.

Individual prices change for countless reasons. Rises and declines in the general price level always indicate changes in the value of money itself. Price changes may be expressed as changes in the price index or as changes in the purchasing power of the dollar.

MEASUREMENT OF CHANGES THROUGH INDEX NUMBERS

Changes in the value of money are measured through the application of a system of index numbers. The U. S. Bureau of Labor Statistics regularly measures the consumer price level, using the prices of some 300 commodities. Due to the great number of prices included, many feel this index is sluggish in its reaction. It is known as the "cost of living" index. The Bureau now uses 1947–49 average prices as a basis. Prices of the same items for another period are expressed as a percentage of the base period price, thus showing changes.[1]

There are many types of averages and many systems of index numbers. Each type of average has a special strength for a certain use, and each is likely to hide a weakness. An unweighted arithmetic average hides extremes. For example, among five persons, four possess 2 dollars each while the fifth has 42 dollars; they average 10 dollars each, but only one has more than 2 dollars. An arithmetic average may also exaggerate price increases, since increases are unlimited as to percentage, but decreases are limited to 100 percent.

Any average may be weighted by taking into consideration either the quantity in which an item is used or its importance. If bread is 10 times as important as iron, multiply the bread base by 10 and add the iron base unchanged. The weighting may also be based on the quantities used. The sum of these weighted averages divided by the sum of the weights gives the weighted average.

---

[1] See pages 69–71.

Index numbers of the aggregative type may be simple or weighted. A simple aggregative index is calculated by adding the total prices actually paid for a group of commodities for a given period, perhaps a year. This total can be compared on a percentage basis with the total of prices for the same items at another period or at the base period.

Weighting is accomplished by the Bureau of Labor Statistics by multiplying the prices paid for each unit of a commodity over a given period by the number of units sold during the given period. A weighted aggregative index avoids the mathematical bias of the simple arithmetical average.

THE EQUATION OF EXCHANGE

Every purchase exemplifies a single equation of exchange. A pair of slacks exchanges for 15 dollars; there is established an equality between 15 dollars and a pair of slacks. Likewise the total amount paid for goods during a period of time equals the sum of the prices of all the units purchased.

Professor Irving Fisher popularized the equation of exchange in algebraic terms as: $MV+M'V'=PT$. In this equation M stands for money and M′ for money substitutes, checks and bank deposits subject to check. V and V′ stand for velocity. P equals the average price paid for all units of goods. T equals the total number of goods transactions.

Changes in any of the factors of this equation of exchange will affect P and account for changes in the general level of prices. By transposition, we have

$$P=\frac{MV+M'V'}{T}$$

Therefore *prices vary directly with the quantity of money and money substitutes, together with the velocity of circulation of each and inversely with the volume of trade.*

QUANTITY THEORY OF MONEY

One of the oldest attempts to explain the causes of general price changes was offered by the "quantity theory of money." It may be simply stated as "other things remaining equal, the value of money varies inversely with its quantity." Subject to much explanation, many exceptions, and circumstantial variations suggested by countless writers, this theory still lies at the base of modern thinking on the causes of changes in the general price level. Individual prices can, and of course do, change for many reasons. Changes in the general price level mean only that there has been a change in the purchasing power of money over goods. Since velocity and the volume of trade seem to change only slowly, does it mean that the quantity of money and the quantity of bank credit chiefly determine the value of money and the general level of prices?

Now if we know that a coin has been cut in half and both halves restamped as complete coins, we immediately want two coins where one sufficed before. Today the Federal Reserve System "creates" money. It expands the money supply as business expands and contracts it as business declines. If the equating is perfect, changes in the quantity of money have no effect on the general price level, since they are related directly to the level of business. To the extent that Government spending correlates with the amount of tax money received and with receipts from bond sales to investors, no changes in the general price level occur. But to the extent that the Government overspends and pays its bills by depositing bonds with the banking system in return for deposit credit against which it may draw checks, it does increase the supply of money just as splitting the coins would. In any one year such deficit spending in the United States has been relatively small, but it is cumulative. A decrease of only 2 or 3 percent per year in money values due to deficit spending cumulates to a diminution of the purchasing power of the dollar by some 20 to 30 percent in a decade.

The effects of an increase in the supply of money or of bank credit for any reason whatever will result in a quickening tempo of everyday spending. It always takes a period of time for the supply of goods to increase in response to greater demand. If the increased tempo of demand is sudden and sharp, prices will increase decidedly. The result is the allocation through the mechanism of the price system of the limited immediately available supply of goods to the highest bidders; more dollars purchase the same amount of goods. Once retail prices have risen, wage demands will result in increased wages and the new price level tends to become permanent. To the extent that an increase in the supply of money is accompanied by an increased output of goods and volume of trade, there is no increase of prices at all.

There are countless other possibilities of change in both supply and demand due to shifts in any one of the factors cited in the equation of exchange. Changes in the general price level are brought about by the interplay of many forces. The quantity theory of money must always be reckoned with, but, in addition, "other things" never "remain equal."

EFFECTS OF PRICE CHANGES

A considerable change in prices brings about a variety of conflicting results. Changing prices do evil to someone, especially if the change is sudden. Fixed income groups suffer immediately when prices rise. Pensioners, recipients of legacies, educational and philanthropic trusts, insurance beneficiaries, and bank savers all suffer at once. Wages and salaries will eventually reflect the higher price level, but they tend to lag behind the upward price movement. Insurance programs and savings plans previously arranged prove inadequate in the long run and must be rearranged.

Although fixed-income groups may welcome price decreases, any recession or depression cuts business initiative and is reflected in a drop in the gross national product. The Government loses anticipated tax revenues, expansion plans of business lag or are abandoned, and there is much unemployment.

Obviously a gently increasing price level may stimulate business, resulting in an overall feeling of confidence in the immediate business future and may lead to actual expansion. Insurance programs can be rearranged to reflect the new conditions and eventually even the payments to pensioners. Under gently increasing prices there is likely to be a feeling of well-being, and worry over the possible dangers of creeping inflation is postponed until tomorrow.

PROPOSALS FOR A FLEXIBLE DOLLAR

Prior to the depression of the 1930's, students of currency problems sought the means of preventing arbitrary, accidental, or mechanical changes in the general price level. When the currency was closely tied to gold, accidental changes in the general price level could occur from changes in the cost of mining gold, from changes in demand for gold as a commodity, and from the continuing increase in supply. A number of proposals were made for stabilizing the purchasing power of the dollar by "compensating" it in various ways and thus divorcing it from the sometimes fortuitous influence of gold.

A *goods dollar* proposed by Irving Fisher was to be tied to a currency based on either gold or inconvertible paper. A *compensated gold dollar* was also proposed, to be adjusted from time to time by making changes in the number of grains of gold in the standard dollar. Value changes in both were to have been made as required by the rise and fall of the index number of prices of a selected list of commodities. A *commodity dollar* based on a paper currency standard would have a value equal to that of an aggregate of selected goods measured by their relative importance in trade. Changes were also to be measured in terms of index numbers.

In these days of central banking systems, the control powers of the Government over banks are used to affect the amount of money in circulation and thus to influence the value of currency through changes in discount rates and bank reserves. The pressure of special interest groups to obtain favorable policies from responsible officials is unceasing. To central bank authorities, at least, the old compensated dollar plans must look simple in retrospect.

PURCHASING-POWER BONDS

A capitalistic system functions best when it is growing, when individuals have confidence in the future, and when they are free to plan and put their ideas into effect. Businessmen like steady prices if not gently firming ones. When prices fall, they worry and tend to lose confidence. If we experience a technological improvement in production methods of 3 percent per year, as we have averaged in many industries in the United States during this century, wages must increase or prices must fall as costs decrease, with many possible combinations of the two.

As productive efficiency increases, labor union members prefer an increase in their own wages to a general decrease in the prices of the products which they make. As purchasing power increases so does demand and, for the reasons shown previously, prices are likely to rise.

It is proposed that the investor be protected from this tendency toward the deterioration of the value of money due to price rises. Such protection could take the form of constant-purchasing-power bonds. These bonds would return to the investor the same purchasing power which he lent. Many a 10-year $1,000 Government bond bought in 1940 for $750 was paid off in 1950. The $250 income therefrom had to be reported as income subject to tax. However, the entire $1,000 would not buy in 1950 what the $750 would have bought in 1940. The constant-purchasing-power bond supposedly would return the same purchasing power originally loaned plus interest. The face value at the time of repayment would be tied to a cost-of-living index.

Unquestionably constant-purchasing-power bonds would attract many purchasers, especially those persons who desire to avoid the rigidity of other types of bonds but who are unwilling to take part in the uncertainties of the stock market. A weakness in such a plan as applied to Government bonds, is that sharp increases in the cost of living might force many bond holders to cash in their holdings. The Treasury then would have to issue "new" money to pay for them through selling its own bonds to the banking system. The consequent increase in the supply of money would encourage greater spending and would likely result in a further increase in the cost of living. The cycle could go on like a dog chasing its tail.

Constant-purchasing-power bonds can be issued also by commercial borrowers. Purchasers who found it necessary to cash them in could do so only in the free market. Free-market purchasers would discount the present value of the bonds to maturity and base their opinions as to the future worth on an appraisal of the issuer of the bonds as well.

VII
ECONOMIC FORECASTING AND STABILIZATION PROCEDURES

FORECASTING

In the Brookings Lectures for 1954, the English economist, John Jewkes refers to his previous writing in which he insisted that economists should not claim the power to predict since there is "no such thing as the economic future. There is only *the* future in which economic factors are bound together, inextricably and quite without hope of separate identification, with the whole universe of forces determining the course of events."

In spite of many warnings, economic forecasting becomes more common. Some forecasters try to save themselves by using obscure words in an attempt to say something significant without being tied down to a statement that can be checked. However, since economic predictions continue on a large scale, there must be a market for them. All of us constantly make decisions dependent on our guesses as to the future, and perhaps it is not surprising that we are prepared to clutch at straws held out by whomsoever, even by the economists.

The economists first moved out of their university halls during the depression years into Government service and the banking field. They became practitioners as well as expounders. Following World War II they moved in considerable numbers into private business.

In the fields of the natural sciences, we label the laboratory men and the teachers as "scientists," while the industrial practitioners are called "engineers." Perhaps something of this sort lies ahead for economics to distinguish between the academicians who develop the theory from the practitioners who apply the art.

BUSINESS CYCLE THEORY

Recessions and depressions have been common since the beginning of the Industrial Revolution. Throughout the 1800's depressions of a regional nature were common enough. Many occasions appeared when there was too much of certain goods in certain areas. When the surplus was used, business renewed itself. These surpluses were temporary and more or less local. Certainly the world remained hungry for all kinds of manufactured products. Historically, recessions seem to move in two cycles, a major cycle of approximately

36 months from valley to peak and a minor cycle of about 18 months within the major cycle.

Numerous economists have sought the reasons underlying changes in the cycle of business. Explanations include money causes, credit causes, over-savings, over-investment, under-consumption, and over-production. Jevons spoke of "sun spots" but was thinking of the weather's reaction on agriculture and not of occult connections. The search for the basic causes of periodic business setbacks continues unabated.

Wesley C. Mitchell thought of business cycles as "self-generating." His explanation has a great appeal. He found four stages generally in the business cycle, each stage logically leading to the next and the cycle continuous and self-perpetuating. If the present position is known, the next can be predicted. The stages are (1) prosperity, (2) crisis, (3) depression, and (4) recovery.

During prosperity production is reasonably balanced, credit is good, production facilities tend to expand, prices are rising, new ventures are encouraged, money is easy, plants and machinery are modernized, and rentals and interest rates based on longer-term contracts rise slowly. Operating costs eventually begin to catch up, interest rates rise, rental contracts run out and are renewed only at higher figures, wages rise, and profits decline.

The consumer resists further price rises, the purchasing power of producers is reduced through slower sales, farm prices decline, business slows up gradually, and banks begin to restrict credit; the crisis stage has arrived. Business loses faith in the price structure, cutrate sales become common, caution is exhibited everywhere, today's purchases are put off because tomorrow's prices may be lower; somewhere a bank crashes and the rout is on.[1]

In the ensuing period of depression, economic prostration prevails. New money is not available for new ventures, and only consumer goods of the most essential nature are produced. The heavy goods producing industries are closed almost entirely, capital structures are reduced, credits are restricted, interest rates fall, and rents are readjusted. Construction work of all kinds is at a practical standstill.

When the maladjustments between wages and prices, credit and capital, and interest and loans have been corrected, economic recovery is possible. Some outside impetus may start the industrial wheels spinning once more. It may be a new invention or series of inventions; new industry may appear; the Government may try pump-priming; or a war may start. Once the stagnation is broken, many factors add to the pickup. Old machinery is replaced, new plant and home construction begins anew, and longstanding con-

[1] Bank failures have been few, however, since 1933.

sumer needs for durables, clothing, and house furnishings are great. The whole cycle starts anew once more.

The above explanation is oversimplified. The depression of the 1930's did not follow the course of earlier cycles. There were various opinions regarding its nature. Some authorities looked upon it as a world depression, a situation of economic maturity wherein many human beings preferred greater leisure to further increase in the possession of manufactured goods. Others expressed the view that the situation was different from other depressions only in that the Government did not take rallying measures soon enough. When such measures were finally taken by the New Deal, recovery lagged because of the lack of confidence on the part of businessmen generally.

The Roosevelt devices included an increase in the money supply, an attempt to raise the price level, a reform of the banking system and the security markets, relief of farmers and of unemployed workers, protection of home owners, strengthening of trade unions, aid to local governments with construction work, and the reduction of personal income inequalities.

Activity did finally return in 1940 and increased generally until 1953–54 when something of a modified breathing spell again appeared. A small industrial stumble had been noted also in 1949. On both of these occasions, however, the built-in stabilizers were in theoretical operation, and they apparently worked as the economic medicine men had predicted. In June of 1955 industrial activity was at an all time high. The built-in stabilizers include old age pensions, unemployment insurance, the insurance of bank deposits, and changes in monetary and fiscal policies.

GOVERNMENT STATISTICS

To paraphrase an old proverb, the better the statistics, the better the forecast. Many kinds of business statistics have been kept by the United States Government agencies for a long time and all series are being constantly improved. Many statistical series have existed enough years to make pattern research worthwhile.

Statisticians and economists generally rely on Government statistics as a source for their research. The official statistics are supplemented by countless statistical series kept by individual industries, by statistics devised and kept up by economic foundations, and by trade associations.

A series of monthly business statistical tables is issued regularly by the United States Department of Commerce in its "Survey of Current Business." They are based on surveys and censuses taken at regular and special intervals and kept current by sampling procedures.

These tables include statistics on national income, new plant and equipment expenditures, farm income and marketing, industrial production, consumer durables output, business sales and inventories, manufacturers' sales, inventories and orders, prices received and paid by farmers, retail prices, consumers' price index, wholesale prices, construction and real estate, domestic trade, employment and population, various finance statistics in a detailed series including such things as the amount of life insurance in force, brokers' loans, international transactions of the United States, transportation and communications, a whole series of statistics by types of industries, and tables on electric power and gas.

The Monthly Labor Review of the United States Department of Labor carries a number of detailed statistical series under six main divisions. Employment and Payrolls, Labor Turnover, Earnings and Hours, Consumer and Wholesale Prices, Work Stoppages, and Building and Construction.

The *Federal Reserve Bulletin* compiled by the Board of Governors of the Federal Reserve System carries detailed monthly statistics on a series of 27 items or categories. This series includes bank reserves, margin requirements, deposits, bank debits and deposits, money in circulation, commercial paper and bankers' acceptances, security prices, real estate credit statistics, short- and intermediate-term consumer credit, and a whole series of business statistics.

The statistical series of other countries were made available in the former League of Nations publications and are now continued by the statistical organization of the United Nations. Actual statistics in reasonable amount and satisfactorily current are available but the *uses* to which they can be put and are being put are the currently important problem.

SHORT-RANGE FORECASTING

The National Bureau of Economic Research, a pioneer institution in the gathering and using of statistics, at its conference in September 1951, defined short-term forecasting as a prediction for a period not more than one or two years into the future. Short-term forecasting tries to measure expectations. Capital outlays and expected sales frequently must be anticipated by businessmen. Consumer anticipations include the expectations to purchase durables, autos, and new houses.

Short-term forecasting relies on indicators, statistical and industrial in type, and more recently has attempted economic model building. But "sound judgment" is a forecasting factor that is never far from the forefront. Forecasting methods include the survey, the interview and the judgment technique. A good short-range forecast must take all methods and techniques into consideration and yet remain flexible enough to permit change as economic conditions actually unfold with time.

LONG-RANGE FORECASTING

Forecasting for the longer term, exceeding one or two years, requires "good hard judgment." Attempts to define the term "judgment," end up with the closely related term "experience," which deals with the past and not with the future. To the extent that hunch or guess enters into a judgment, to that extent is the forecast personal to him who makes the prophecy.

Long-range forecasters must use the services of the population expert for information as to the rate of change and growth in the population. From him they get some idea of the numbers to be found in the labor force on a future date, the number of new families likely to be formed yearly, the adequacy of the housing that will be available, and the general change in demand for food and manufactures. Some forecast of new inventions and processes is important. An extension of the increase in manufacturing efficiency on the basis of past experience can be worked out. The calculation of the length of the future workweek and the forecast of future uses of leisure time are essential. Leisure time generates its own set of requirements for products.

The forecaster also needs the services of the actuary in determining the number of older and old people to be cared for at future dates. He must also calculate the level of social security benefits likely to prevail and must estimate the group's willingness to take part in the labor force. World forces and world events will also affect the long-range forecast. Long-range economic forecasting, however, can be couched in much more general terms than can the short-range statistical prediction

THE ECONOMIC REPORT OF THE PRESIDENT

An important aid to economic forecasting is the Economic Report of the President. The Employment Act of 1946 has as its stated purpose to foster and promote free competitive enterprise and general welfare conditions under which there will be afforded useful employment opportunities and to promote maximum employment, production, and purchasing power. Under this statute as revised, the President sends the Economic Report of the President to the Congress each January. This report covers the levels of employment, production, and purchasing power prevailing; current and foreseeable trends; a review of economic conditions affecting employment during the preceding year; a program for carrying out the policy declared in the act; and such recommendations for legislation as the President may deem necessary or desirable. The President relies on a Council of Economic Advisers for background information on which to make his report. The statistical appendix is quite detailed.

When the President's Report is received by the Congress, it is referred to the Joint Economic Committee where it is examined and studied by the Committee's own economic staff. Upon completion of the staff study, the Joint Economic Committee must itself send a report to the full Congress not later than 1 May of each year that opens a regular session. This report gives the Committee's own estimate of the economic situation.

The Council of Economic Advisors prepares a monthly bulletin of statistical tables called *Economic Indicators*.[1] A short interpretation is offered of the meaning of any change in a statistical table appearing since the last bulletin. These statistics cover Gross National Product, Prices, Employment and Wages, Production and Business Activity, Purchasing Power and Credit, Money and Federal Finance.

These periodical surveys of the economy by the executive and legislative branches of the Government, together with their recommendations for improving and stabilizing the economy, may be termed economic forecasting. In 1954 the Joint Economic Committee, through its staff director, issued a long-range forecast, "Potential Economic Growth of the United States During the Next Decade." Trade associations, planning groups of business, and individual businesses are more and more concerning themselves with their own long-range forecasts.

---

[1] Economic Indicators are treated more fully in chapter IX.

VIII
NATIONAL INCOME ACCOUNTING[1]

Compilation of national income statistics was initiated in 1932 in the United States in response to Senate Resolution of the 72nd Congress. Originally Congress directed the preparation of measures of the national income, its industrial origin, and its distribution in the form of wages, profits, and other types of payments. The initial report appeared in 1934 as Senate Document 124, 72nd Congress, 2nd Session. National income estimates have been published annually since that date.

During the past twenty years national income statistics have become firmly established in many countries as basic tools of economic analysis. These statistics provide material equally essential for the production and marketing programs of business and for furthering the knowledge requisite for the formulation and development of Government economic programs. They were particularly valuable during the war years for the establishment of goals designed to maximize total production, for the necessary diversion of production to war purposes, and for supplementing the income measurements in the calculation of the inflationary pressures being generated.

NATIONAL PRODUCT: THE FLOW OF GOODS AND SERVICES

Total output is measured from two principal points of view: as the summation of final products produced by the economy; and as the summation of costs incurred in producing those products.

The gross national product measures the Nation's output of goods and services in terms of its market value. Expressed in current prices, this series reflects the total dollar value of production; expressed in constant dollars, to eliminate the influence of price changes, it provides an overall index of the physical volume of goods and services produced. The gross national product is broken down to show its disposition among broad groups of users—consumers, business, Government, and foreign countries (fig. 6).

[1] The material in this chapter is taken rather literally from *National Income*, 1951 edition, *A Supplement to the Survey of Current Business*, U. S. Department of Commerce, Washington, D. C., GPO, 1951.

GROSS NATIONAL PRODUCT OR EXPENDITURE

According to current estimates, gross national product rose $1.3 billion (seasonally adjusted annual rate) between the fourth quarter of 1955 and the first quarter of 1956. Consumption expenditures increased $1.6 billion and government purchases rose $0.2 billion, while gross private domestic investment declined $0.8 billion.

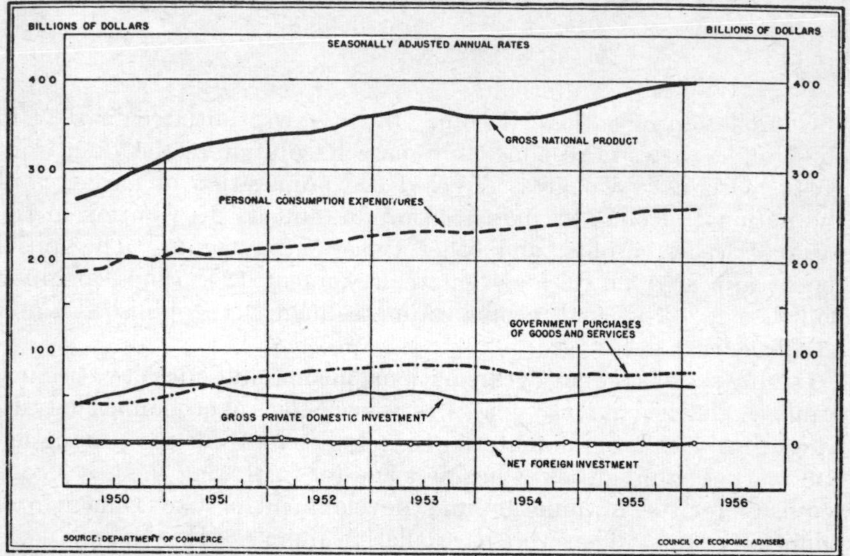

SOURCE: Economic Indicators, May 1956.

Figure 6.

NATIONAL INCOME: EARNINGS FROM PRODUCTION

Total output is also measured in terms of the factor costs of producing it, by the national income; i. e., the aggregate earnings of labor and property which arise from current production. National income differs from gross national product in that it is computed after deduction of indirect business taxes and depreciation charges and other allowances for business consumption of durable capital goods.

National income is broken down by distributive shares, by industry of origin, and by legal form of organization. Distributive shares represent a classification of earnings according to the forms in which they accrue to the citizens—compensation of employees, profits of corporate and unincorporated enterprises, net interest, and the rental incomes of persons. Industry of origin indicates the use of economic resources and the contribution to total output by each of a number of industrial subdivisions as measured by income originating in the respective industries.

Legal form of organization shows an important special aspect of the institutional structure of the economy—the portions of total economic activity conducted by various types of productive units, including corporations, sole proprietorships and partnerships, other private business enterprises, Government and Government enterprises, and households and institutions. These "summary accounts," of course, require the keeping of many individual accounts on which they are based. These individual accounts include current income and outlay accounts for business, for persons, for Government, and a consolidated savings and investment account for the economy as a whole.

PERSONAL INCOME: RECEIPTS OF CONSUMERS

The personal account covers the activities of the consuming public. Personal income is generally coordinated for economic analysis with gross national product and national income. On the one hand it gives the current income received by persons from all sources, including transfers from the Government and from business. On the other hand, it indicates the disposition of personal income for consumption, taxes, and saving.

NATIONAL INCOME STATISTICS; CONCEPTUAL FRAMEWORK

As noted, the purpose of national income research is to provide information on the outcome of economic activity through comprehensive measures of the size, composition, and use of national output. National income statistics have been used to an increasing extent to facilitate an understanding of the factors which determine the product of economic activity. More and more, national income statistics have been designed with the dual objective of measuring the national output and of placing it against the background of the transactions which underlie its production and distribution (fig. 7).

National income statistics provide the basic statistical framework required for the study of long-term economic trends and of business fluctuations and for the formulation of business and Government economic policies. These data are needed when the automatic working of the market mechanism cannot be fully relied upon and steps must be taken to modify its functioning. The mitigation of business cycles in times of peace and the current planning for national defense are important instances in which an understanding of the economic mechanism, such as is facilitated by the use of national income statistics, is the prerequisite to intelligent action designed to improve its operation. Again, even when no influencing of economic events is under consideration, the businessman wants to gauge the probable market for his output and to obtain a more rational basis for determining his policies. In addition, the tax administrator is interested, since he must estimate governmental revenues.

NATIONAL INCOME

According to preliminary estimates, national income rose about $1½ billion (seasonally adjusted annual rate) between the fourth quarter of 1955 and the first quarter of 1956. Increases in compensation of employees and in other incomes were offset in part by decreases in farm and corporate income.

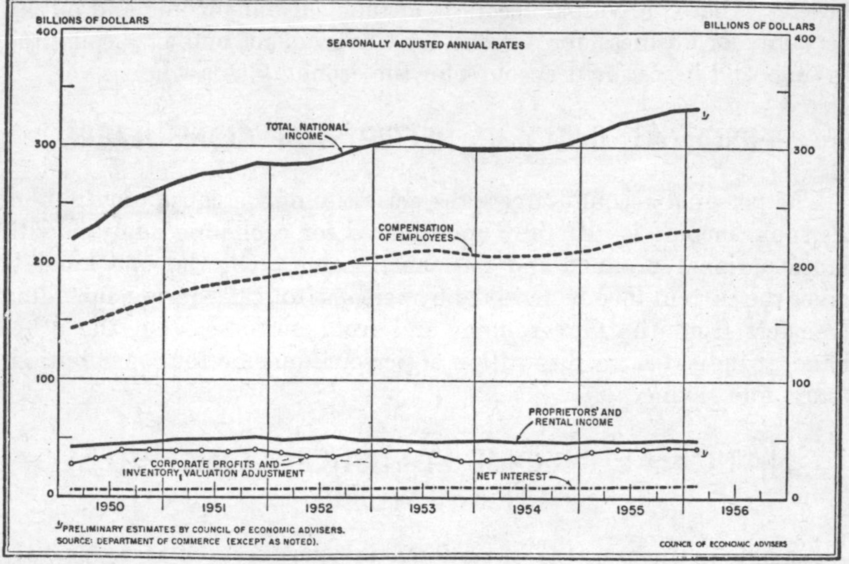

SOURCE: Economic Indicators, May 1956.

Figure 7.

ECONOMIC ACCOUNTING SYSTEM

The production and distribution of the Nation's output necessitate countless transactions of buying and selling, hiring labor, investing capital, renting property, paying taxes, and other operations. The records of these transactions kept by business, consumer, and governmental units reflect the most concrete manifestations of the Nation's economic life, but they must be summarized into a limited number of significant categories. This is the basic task of the national economic accounting system. The accounting system underlying the United States estimates is based upon a division of the economy into major sectors. A national income and product account is first established, which provides measures of total national output (table 3).

ADDITIONAL INCOME AND PRODUCT ACCOUNTS

Next, accounts are set up for each of the four main sectors of the economy—business, consumers, Government, and foreign payments and trade (foreign investment). In addition to showing the portions of national output originating in each of them, they are designed to depict the economic structure in terms of the interrelated transactions of the four major economic groups. These trace the transactions determining the current income of each of the sectors, the part of that income used up, and the part devoted to saving. The sector account for business is in essence a consolidated profit and loss account for the business system as a whole. For the other sectors, the accounts represent current receipt and expenditure accounts, in conformance with the nonprofitmaking character of their transactions.

DEFINITIONS OF CONCEPTS AND TERMS

National income is the aggregate earnings of labor and property which arise from the current production of goods and services by the Nation's economy. Thus it measures the total factor costs of the goods and services produced by the economy. Earnings are recorded in the forms in which they accrue to residents, inclusive of taxes on those earnings: compensation of employees, the profits of corporate and unincorporated enterprises, net interest, and the rental income flowing to persons.

Table 3. National Income and Product Account, 1955

(Balance sheet, billions of dollars)

Wages and supplements[1]		221.3	Statistical discrepancy	−0.1
Income of unincorporated enterprises		38.4	Net National Product	354.9
Rental income		10.7	Capital consumption allowances (depreciation)	32.3
Corporate profits and inventory valuation adj		41.4	Gross National Product[2]	387.2
Corporate taxes	21.8		Personal consumption expenditures	252.3
Undistributed profits	10.4		Gross private domestic investment	59.3
Dividends	11.2		Net foreign investment	−.4
Inv. val. adj	−2.0		Government purchase of goods and services	75.9
Net interest		10.5	Statistical discrepancy	−.1
National Income		322.3	Gross National Product[2]	387.2
Indirect business taxes		31.9		
Business transfer payments		1.2		

SOURCE: [1] Data in this column from table 4.
[2] From *Economic Indicators*, May 1956.

(Discrepancies in addition due to rounding)

Gross national product is the market value of the output of goods and services produced by the Nation's economy, before deduction of depreciation charges and other allowances for business and institutional consumption of durable capital goods. Gross national product comprises the purchases of goods and services by consumers and Government, gross private domestic investment, and net foreign investment.

Net national product is the market value of the net output of goods and services produced by the Nation's economy. All business products used up by business are excluded. Net national product comprises the purchases of goods and services by consumers and Government, net private domestic investment, and net foreign investment.

Personal income is the current income received by persons from all sources, inclusive of transfers from Government and business, but exclusive of transfers among persons. Individuals, the owners of unincorporated enterprises, nonprofit institutions, private trust funds, and private pension and welfare funds are classified as "persons." Personal income is measured as the sum of wage and salary receipts, other labor income, proprietors' and rental income, interest and dividends, and transfer payments.

Disposable income is the income remaining to persons after deduction of personal tax and nontax payments to general government.

TRENDS IN THE UNITED STATES ECONOMY AS TRACED BY THE NATIONAL INCOME STATISTICS SERIES

The national income statistics series since 1929 shows the tremendous growth of the United States economy. The population increased by more than a third, from 122 million in 1929 to 165 million in 1955. The number of persons engaged in production rose in roughly similar proportion. This work force is now equipped with better machinery and plant facilities and is better educated and trained. These factors together with advanced scientific knowledge have resulted in a vastly increased flow of goods and services and a wide array of new products.

The gross national product amounted to $387.2 billion in 1954, as compared with $104 billion in 1929. Gross national product was estimated in mid-1956 to be running at the annual rate of $400 billion. Prices are currently much higher than in 1929, but there is still tremendous growth. Prices in 1956 are more than 50 percent above 1929, but the physical volume of output, measured by the gross national product in constant dollars, has risen 80 percent. In terms of real output per capita, the increase amounts to 45 percent. The long-term rate of growth in national production, provided by the average annual percentage increase in constant-dollar gross national product, from 1929 to 1955 averaged slightly more than 2.75 percent per year expansion in the real volume of output. This growth reflects the increase in manpower resources as well, but the advance in produc-

Table 4. Relation of Gross National Product, National Income, and Personal Income, 1955

(Billions of dollars)

	Gross national product	Net national product	National income	Personal income
Capital consumption allowances (depreciation and obsolescence).	32.3	GNP less depreciation.	NNP less indirect business taxes and transfers.	
Indirect business taxes	31.9	31.9		
Business transfer payments	1.2	1.2		
Statistical discrepancy	−0.1	−0.1		
Corporate profits and inventory valuation adjustment.	41.4	41.4	41.4	NI less undistributed profits and corporate taxes.
Corporate taxes 21.8				
Undistributed profits 10.4				
Dividends 11.2				11.2.
Inventory valuation adjustment −2.0				
Interest	10.5	10.5	10.5	10.5.
Rents	10.7	10.7	10.7	10.7.
Unincorporated net income (business, professions, farms)	38.4	38.4	38.4	38.4.
Wages and supplements	221.3	221.3	221.3	221.3.
Plus:				
Government transfer payments.				16.0.
Net interest paid by Government.				5.0.
Business transfers				1.2.
Less:				
Social security payments.				11.0.
Total	387.2	354.9	322.3	303.3.

SOURCE: Department of Commerce, Survey of Current Business, February 1955. (Revised totals in July issue.)

(Discrepancies in addition are due to rounding.)

Personal Income, 303.3 less personal taxes, 33.9 equals *Disposable Income*, 269.4.

Disposable Income, 269.4 less personal savings, 17.1 equals *Personal Consumption Expenditures*, 252.3.

tion has outstripped this increase by a wide margin. There are sizable gains in productivity per unit of manpower utilized. The number of persons engaged in production in private industries rose about 1 percent per year on the average. An average annual rate of growth in real private product per person engaged averaged approximately 1.75 percent since 1929. During the same period the number of hours worked per week was reduced by about 10 percent.

The percentage distribution of the gross national product for two years, 1929 and 1950, in current dollars was:

	1929	1950
Personal consumption expenditures	75. 9	68. 5
Gross private domestic investment	15. 2	17. 3
Net foreign investment	. 7	—. 8
Government purchases of goods and services	8. 2	15. 0
	100. 0	100. 0

SHIFTS IN THE USE OF NATIONAL OUTPUT

There were significant changes in the disposition of the gross national product among major groups of users between 1929 and 1950 and in the composition of purchases by each of these groups. All domestic sectors of the economy shared in the increased volume of production. Net foreign investment, which measures net purchases of United States output by the rest of the world, was the only principal component of national product to show decline since 1929. Government purchases of goods and services measured in current dollars almost doubled. Personal consumption expenditures dropped, reflecting in part the increase in Government expenditures. The proportion of the value of output going into domestic and foreign investment was nearly the same.

Although the proportion going to consumers dropped slightly, the absolute volume of goods and services purchased for personal consumption increased nearly 40 percent in real consumption per capita. Expenditures for consumer durable goods increased from 12 percent of total consumer spending in 1929 to more than 15 percent in 1950. The share going to nondurable consumer commodities also increased, but the proportion spent on services dropped considerably. There was a lag, however, in rents and household utility charges. The period was characterized by an increased reliance on private automobile transportation and an expanding use of household appliances. The employment of domestic servants declined.

There was a large increase in the relative importance of the manufacturing industries since 1929. This increase is reflected in a somewhat lesser but definite percentage increase in the wholesale and retail trade industries. Earnings in the real estate industry, especially on residential property, were relatively depressed. The income of banking and other financial industries suffered from the halving of the average interest rates and the marked shift from external financing of business investment to financing out of retained earnings.

Interest rates and rental incomes increased somewhat between 1950 and 1955. From 1951 to 1953 a greater percentage of production went to defense goods. A recession in 1953–54 indicated the change-over once more from defense production to more complete consumer production.

Table 5. Gross National Product in Current and Constant Value Dollars

(Selected years—billions of dollars)

Year	GNP current dollars	GNP 1954 dollars	Year	GNP current dollars	GNP 1954 dollars
1910	36. 7	100. 0	1940	100. 6	205. 9
1915	42. 1	112. 0	1945	213. 5	311. 8
1920	85. 0	123. 0	1950	285. 1	318. 5
1925	88. 0	155. 0	1953	364. 9	368. 5
1930	91. 1	164. 3	1954	357. 2	357. 2
1935	72. 5	153. 0			

SOURCE: Selected.

IX
ECONOMIC INDICATORS

The economy of a large industrial country is so complex that the judgments of individuals regarding its performance have only a limited value. There are numerous particular trends, some of which may seem to be in conflict with others, and the individual often sees the whole picture from the standpoint of that geographical area and portion of the economy that affect him most seriously. Thus the Idaho farmer may view the economic outlook differently from the Government employee in Washington, D. C.; and the automobile salesman in Boston, differently from the nuclear scientist in Oak Ridge.

One of the most useful publications for helping the individual to gain a better view of the economy as a whole as well as of its particular trends is the monthly statistical report entitled *Economic Indicators*. It grew out of the charts and tables constructed in the staff studies of the Council of Economic Advisers. As the knowledge of these charts and tables spread, Congressmen desired copies for themselves. *Economic Indicators* was authorized as a monthly publication in 1949 and was made available for sale to the public. It has become, says one economist, "the most sought-after document . . . on the current status of the economy of any document available in Washington." [1] It is prepared by the Council of Economic Advisers and is issued for a congressional committee, the Joint Committee on the Economic Report.

Each issue is made up of six major series dealing with Total Output, Income and Spending; Employment, Unemployment, and Wages; Production and Business Activity; Prices; Currency, Credit, and Security Markets; and Federal Finance. Each of these is made up of two or more parts for a total of 32 series.

TOTAL OUTPUT, INCOME, AND SPENDING

The first series develops ten individual charts and accompanying statistical tables on The Nation's Income, Expenditure, and Saving; Gross National Product or Expenditure; National Income; Sources of Personal Income; Disposition of Personal Income; Per Capita Disposable Income; Farm Income, Corporate Profits, Gross Private Domestic Investment; and Expenditures for New Plant and Equipment.

---

[1] M. R. Gainsbrugh, *Economic Indicators*, ICAF lecture, 2 September 1954. L55-13, p. 2.

A sufficient general description of the material on which this series is based is given in the preceding chapter on National Income Accounting. Each graph is headed by a short interpretation of trend since the last monthly report. Gross National Product or Expenditure and National Income from the May 1956 issue of *Economic Indicators* are shown as figures 6 and 7. Additional historical and descriptive materials covering all sections of this report, and upon which this chapter is based, may be found in the "1955 Historical and Descriptive Supplement to Economic Indicators" prepared for the Joint Economic Committee by the Committee staff and the Office of Statistical Standards, Bureau of the Budget.

EMPLOYMENT, UNEMPLOYMENT, AND WAGES

The second series, Employment, Unemployment, and Wages, develops five monthly indicators showing Status of the Labor Force, Nonagricultural Employment, Average Weekly Hours—Selected Industries, Average Hourly Earnings—Selected Industries, Average Weekly Earnings—Selected Industries (fig. 8).

EMPLOYMENT, UNEMPLOYMENT, AND WAGES
STATUS OF THE LABOR FORCE

Total employment (inclusive of agriculture) rose by about 900,000 between March and April and unemployment declined by about ¼ million. The rise in employment was somewhat larger than usual, and the decline in unemployment about usual, for this time of year.

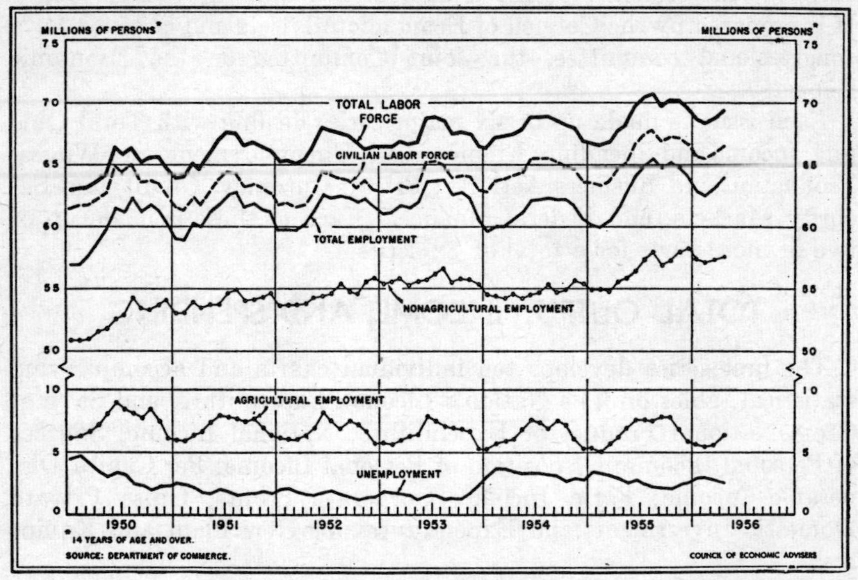

SOURCE: Economic Indicators, May 1956.

Figure 8.

Status of the labor force. Each month, the Bureau of the Census of the Department of Commerce publishes estimates of the labor force and of total employment and unemployment. Detail is presented on the characteristics of employed and unemployed persons, such as age, sex, color, marital status, and veteran status. Employed persons are further classified as those employed in agriculture and in nonagricultural pursuits by class of worker, by broad occupation groups, and by hours worked during the survey week, and by reasons for part-time work. Duration of unemployment is shown for the unemployed. The estimates are obtained by means of a sample survey of households representing all persons in the continental United States except those living in institutions, such as prisons or homes for the aged. All persons 14 years and over in the sample households are classified as employed, unemployed, or not in the labor force for the calendar week ending nearest the 15th of the month. The sum of the employed and the unemployed constitutes the "civilian labor force." Housewives, students, retired or disabled persons, those doing less than 15 hours of unpaid family work, and the voluntarily idle are classified as "not in the labor force." The estimates of unemployment are used as a current indicator of the general health of the economy.

Nonagricultural employment. Current monthly series on employment in nonagricultural establishments with related information on hours and earnings, is prepared by the Bureau of Labor Statistics. Employment estimates are published for more than 200 separate industry groups and subgroups as well as 8 major industry divisions (manufacturing, mining, trade, etc.). Employment figures represent the total number of persons employed in nonagricultural establishments in the continental United States during a specified payroll period which is that ending nearest the 15th of the month. Employed persons include all those who worked during or received pay for any part of the payroll period, including part-time, full-time, temporary and permanent employees. Workers on an establishment's payroll who are on paid sick leave, paid holiday or paid vacation, or who work a part of a specified pay period and are unemployed or on strike during the other part are considered employed. Persons are not considered employed who are laid off, on leave without pay, or on strike for the entire pay period. Proprietors, the self-employed and unpaid family workers, and domestic workers in households are included among the employed.[2] Government employment statistics refer to civilian employees only but include employees of the Federal, State, and local governments. Current employment statistics are widely used as a timely indicator of changes in economic activity in various sectors of the economy.

[2] The determination of employed varies for different purposes.

Average weekly hours—selected industries. The average hour figures are obtained by dividing the number of production and related workers (or nonsupervisory workers in industries other than mining and manufacturing) into the total man-hours reported for each industry. The average hours are normally less than scheduled hours because of such factors as absenteeism, labor turnover, part-time work, and stoppages. Changes in hours worked supplement the information on employment, since hours worked frequently are affected even before employment by changes in economic activity.

Average hourly earnings—selected industries. The payroll figures on which these averages are based are reported before deductions for taxes, social insurance, etc. They include pay for sick leave, holidays, and vacations taken but exclude retroactive pay and bonuses, unless earned and paid regularly each pay period. Earnings in 1954 prices are the average hourly earnings adjusted for changes in purchasing power as determined by the Consumer Price Index. These figures are widely used in collective bargaining, in "escalator" long-term sales contracts (such as labor costs for equipment which takes a number of months or years to build), and in general economic analysis. The fact that large establishments predominate in the BLS sample may affect somewhat the level of the average earnings for some industries but has no measurable effect on the trends in average hourly earnings.

Average weekly earnings—selected industries. Average weekly earnings are obtained by multiplying average weekly hours and average hourly earnings for each industry. They come closer than the hourly earnings to measuring what the worker has to spend, since they are affected by changes in the length of the workweek. They do not represent take-home pay, since no deductions have been made for income and social security taxes, group insurance, occupational supplies, union dues, or other payroll deductions.

PRODUCTION AND BUSINESS ACTIVITY

The third series, Production and Business Activity, develops seven monthly indicators showing Industrial Production, Production of Selected Manufactures, Weekly Indicators of Production, New Construction, Housing Starts and Applications for Financing, Sales and Inventories (Manufacturing and Trade), and Merchandise Exports and Imports (fig. 9).

Industrial production. The Index of Industrial Production is designed to measure changes in the physical volume or quantity of output of manufactures and minerals. (See table 7.) It does not register changes in the value of such production, nor does it include

PRODUCTION AND BUSINESS ACTIVITY

INDUSTRIAL PRODUCTION

The index of industrial production (seasonally adjusted) is estimated at 142 (1947–49=100) in April, 1 point above the revised March index, and 2 points below the all-time high of last December.

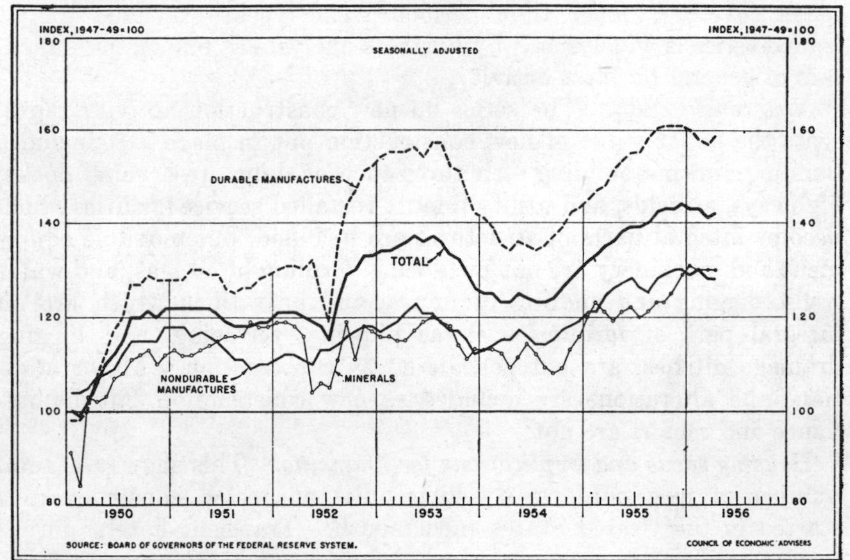

SOURCE: Economic Indicators, May 1956.

Figure 9.

other productive activities often regarded as industrial; i. e., construction and public utilities. The manufacturing and mining industries covered by the index produce about one-third of the value of the total output of goods and services in the United States. Both annual and monthly data are utilized. The total index of industrial production is most widely used as a business barometer. It is used with related data on employment, inventories, trade, prices, and other economic variables, in analyzing short-run and long-run developments in the economy. Many companies make continuing studies of their own output and sales figures in relation to the output movements of the industry.

Production of selected manufactures. The table on Production of Selected Manufactures presents index figures for nine of the major components of the index of manufactures. This series includes durable manufactures, nondurable manufactures, and the consumer durable goods index. The index of consumer durable goods is essentially an index of the volume of factory output of finished consumer durable commodities. (See page 77.)

Weekly indicators of production. The weekly series is for a number of selected indicators—steel, electric power, bituminous coal, freight loaded, paper-board produced, and cars and trucks. The series is useful as current measures, available more promptly than monthly or annual figures but are subject to erratic movements not shown in series covering longer time periods. The weekly revenue freight loaded series is widely used by business analysts as one of the indicators of general business activity.

New construction. The series on new construction activity represents the dollar value of new construction put in place. It includes building and nonbuilding structures such as dams, reservoirs, docks, highways, airfields, and utility lines. Installed service facilities which become integral parts of structures are included, but movable equipment and machinery are not included. Drilling of oil, gas, and water wells, digging and shoring of mines, and operations which are an integral part of farming such as plowing, terracing, and digging drainage ditches, are not considered as construction. Major additions and alterations are included as new construction, but maintenance and repairs are not.

Housing starts and applications for financing. This shows the total number of new nonfarm dwelling units on which construction is started in the United States each month. Transient hotels, dormitories, trailers, houseboats, sheds, shacks, and temporary World War II housing built by the Government are not included. Data compiled for housing starts are used in the preparation of estimates for the series on new construction. They serve as an important guide in the formulation of national housing policy and as an indicator of a substantial part of all building activity and related economic trends.

Sales and inventories—manufacturing and trade. Total sales and inventories for manufacturing and trade are estimated monthly by the Office of Business Economics, Department of Commerce, by summing the estimates computed separately for manufacturing, retail trade, and wholesale trade. The sales estimates include all business receipts of the reporting companies or establishments, not just receipts from sale of merchandise. In general, the inventory estimates are based on the values carried on the books of the reporting panels. The current estimates are adjusted for seasonal variation. The monthly sales and inventories are important economic indicators, reflecting the level of economic activity at the three major stages of the distributive process. Sales reflect the demand for goods and services at these three stages and constitute a basic measure of the state of business for the periods covered. Inventories reflect the difference between output and consumption in the economy. In most past periods of business decline and recovery, the rate of inventory depletion or accumulation has accounted for a large part of the aggregate change in overall economic activity.

Merchandise exports and imports. The monthly figures on exports give the value of merchandise (except in-transit merchandise) shipped from the United States to foreign countries. Exports of Alaska, Hawaii, and Puerto Rico to foreign countries are shown as United States exports. Shipments between the United States and its territories and possessions are not regarded as exports or imports. Both Government and non-Government exports are included. The former include mutual security program, military and economic aid, and Department of the Army civilian supply shipments, but shipments to United States Armed Forces and diplomatic missions abroad for their own use are excluded.

The monthly figures on imports give the value of "general imports" into the United States; that is, merchandise released from customs custody immediately upon arrival plus merchandise entered into customs bonded warehouses on arrival. As in the case of exports, Alaska, Hawaii and Puerto Rico are included with continental United States and both Government and non-Government shipments are recorded. Similarly the exclusions with respect to in-transit shipments, gold and silver, and low-value items apply to imports as well. Imports are valued at the foreign or export value, whichever is higher.

The overall series provides accurate monthly indicators of the movement of merchandise exports and imports. It does not distinguish between Government and non-Government transactions.

PRICES

The fourth series, Prices, includes only three monthly indicators—Consumer Prices, Wholesale Prices, and Prices Received and Paid by Farmers.

Consumer prices. The Consumer Price Index compiled by the Bureau of Labor Statistics is a measure of changes in prices of goods and services purchased by families of urban wage earners and salaried clerical workers. The goods and services included in the index are those required to maintain the level of living characteristics of such families in the year ending June 1952. These families represent about 64 percent of all people living in urban places and about 40 percent of the total United States population.

The index is based upon prices collected on about 300 items. Current prices for the 300 items are collected regularly from a list of stores and service establishments in 46 cities. Detailed specifications are used so that prices are obtained for articles of the same quality in successive price periods, insofar as possible. Prices are also collected on such items as physicians' and dentists' fees, hospital rates, and beauty parlor services. Sales and excise taxes are included in the retail prices for commodities on which they are imposed. Property taxes are included in the cost of home ownership and implicitly included in rental costs. The index does not include income taxes or social security taxes. Prices are collected at intervals, ranging from every month to every fourth month. For rents, foods and a few other important items, prices are collected monthly (fig. 10).

Wholesale prices. The Wholesale Price Index is based on price quotations for approximately 2,000 commodities selected to represent all commodities sold on primary markets in the United States. All types of commodities from raw materials to fabricated products are included in the index. The majority of the quotations are producers' prices rather than wholesalers' prices. The prices relate to a particular day of the month—usually Tuesday of the week containing the 15th. The index is designed to measure real price changes; that is, changes which are not occasioned by changes in quality, quantity, or terms of sale. It is not designed to measure changes in manufactures' average realized prices which are affected by product mix and terms of sale as well as by price movements.

PRICES

CONSUMER PRICES

The average of consumer prices rose fractionally in March. Food prices increased 0.2 percent, following a 5-month decline. Prices of all other major groups, except transportation and housing, also increased.

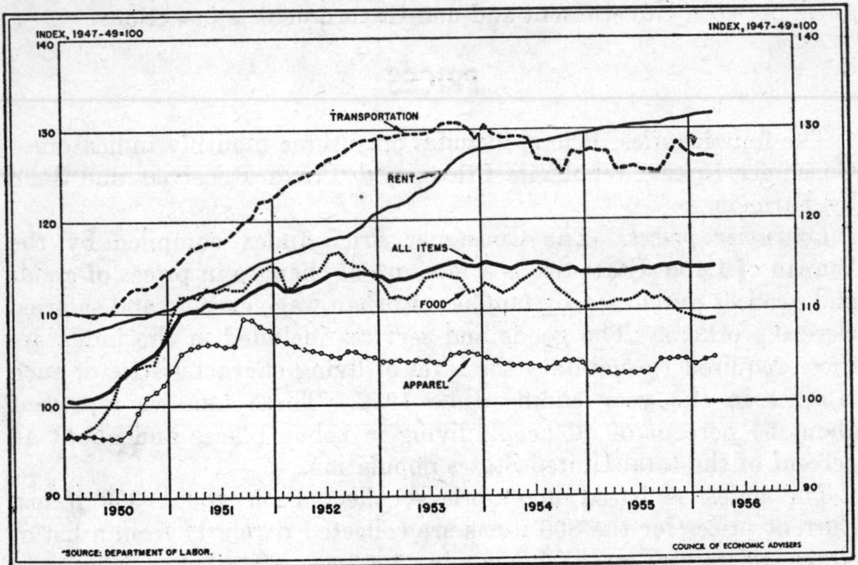

Source: Economic Indicators, May 1956.

Figure 10

Prices received and paid by farmers. The Index of Prices Paid by Farmers for Commodities and Services, including interest, taxes, and wage rates, commonly called the Parity Index, is computed by the Agricultural Marketing Service of the Department of Agriculture. It is composed of five major groups: prices paid for items used in family living, prices paid for items used in farm production, interest on indebtedness secured by farm mortgages, taxes on farm real estate, and rates of wages paid hired farm labor.

The index is a measure of the changes in prices paid by farm families for certain commodities and services used in family living and farm production. This index is frequently compared with the Consumer Price Index to compare the movement of retail prices as they affect farmers and urban workers, respectively. The Parity Index is used to compute parity prices by relating it to prices received by farmers for specific commodities in the base period. Agricultural support programs are in many cases based on these parity prices. The base period is 1910–14 as set by law.

The Index of Prices Received by Farmers is computed by the Agricultural Marketing Service of the Department of Agriculture as a measure of the change from month to month in average prices of farm products. It is based on prices for 52 commodities which account for about 92 percent of the total cash receipts from marketings of all farm commodities. In addition to the overall index for "all farm products," indexes are prepared for livestock and livestock products and for 13 subgroups. The Index of Prices Received by Farmers measures changes in prices at the point of first sale and is based on average prices for all grades of a given commodity. It is used as a measure of changes in average prices received by farmers for commodities sold in local markets and in the computation of adjusted base-period prices, which are needed in calculating parity prices under the formula prescribed.

The Parity Ratio is computed by dividing the Index of Prices Received by Farmers by the Index of Prices Paid. It measures whether the prices farmers receive for farm products are, on the average, higher or lower in relation to the prices they pay for goods and services than they were in the base period, 1910–14.

CURRENCY, CREDIT, AND SECURITY MARKETS

The fifth series, Currency, Credit, and Security Markets, develops five monthly indicators—Currency and Deposits; Bank Loans, Investments, and Reserves; Consumer Credit; Bond Yields and Interest Rates; and Stock Prices. The series measures the supply of several

types of assets of the highest liquidity, which have in varying degrees attributes associated with "money."

Currency and deposits. The table on Currency and Deposits covers privately held deposits and currency and deposits to the credit of the Federal Government. The data on deposits and currency permit an adequate measurement of the level and general trend of the supply of these types of highly liquid assets. Changes in the supply of these assets are important factors affecting the functioning of the economic system (fig. 11).

Bank loans, investments, and reserves. Of the approximately 14,000 commercial banks in the United States, just under 7,000 are members of the Federal Reserve System but account for about 85 percent of the total loans and investments of commercial banks. Mutual savings banks, savings and loan associations, and other banking institutions which do not receive demand deposits are not included in this series. The category of "loans" reported for all commercial banks covers all loans and discounts including open market paper. "Required reserve balances" for member banks are the minimum amount of deposits required to be maintained by member banks at their respective Federal Reserve Banks, measured as a percent of deposit liability.

Consumer credit. The consumer credit table contains estimates of short-term and intermediate-term consumer credit in total and by major types. Consumer credit is defined as "all credit used to finance the purchase of commodities and services for personal consumption or to refinance debts originally incurred for such purposes." Credit covers both loans and sales involving deferred payment. Personal consumption is defined to exclude consumption not only by business but by nonprofit organizations. The estimates exclude home-mortgage credit, traditionally considered separately. Installment credit is that scheduled to be repaid in two or more payments. "Automobile paper" and "other consumer goods paper" includes credit for the purchase of, and secured by, such goods regardless of whether originating as loans or as credit sales and regardless of whether the paper is held by a merchant or a financial institution. Repair and modernization loans include such loans held by financial institutions but not by merchants. Personal installment loans are loans by financial institutions for all other consumer purposes, such as to consolidate debts and to pay medical or educational expenses. Consumers "noninstallment credit" includes charge accounts, single-payment loans, and service credit (including hospitals, doctors, utilities, and service establishments).

Bond yields and interest rates. The tabulation of Bond Yields and Interest Rates covers 3-month treasury bills, taxable Government bonds, high-grade municipal bonds, corporate bonds, and prime commercial paper. This information is useful as a measure of the cost of open-market, short-term credit available to large business borrowers of the highest credit standing.

Stock prices. Stock-price indexes measure average price movement of the 265 or more active common stocks listed on the New York Stock Exchange. This is a moderately sensitive weekly index presented in categories roughly comparable with those used in other series.

FEDERAL FINANCE

The last series, Federal Finance, develops only two monthly indicators—Budget Receipts and Expenditures and Cash Receipts from and Payments to the Public.

Budget receipts and expenditures. Budget receipts represent the income of the Federal Government and are derived mostly from taxes, but they also include fees, fines, proceeds from the sale of property, and other miscellaneous items. Budget expenditures represent payments for Government programs including capital outlays, purchases of goods and services, transfer payments, grants to states, and certain payments to Federal trust funds. Transactions of trust funds are excluded from budget receipts and expenditures. Data on budget receipts and expenditures reflect the financial transactions of all Government-owned funds and therefore serve as an important indicator of executive and legislative budget policy. The relationship between the receipts and expenditure figures serves as the major determinant of increases or decreases in the public debt. This series has important limitations: business activity may be influenced by Government financial operations long before such operations are reflected in the figures on budget expenditures or receipts. Some of the economic impact is reflected at the stage when contracts for goods and services are let. Federal guaranties and insurance of private loans have an impact on economic activity although they have a relatively minor effect on budget receipts or expenditures. The operations of the trust funds and Government-sponsored enterprises play an important role which is not reflected in budget figures.

Cash receipts from and payments to the public. These data present information on the flow of money between the public and the Federal Government as a whole. The excess of Federal cash receipts or payments is sometimes referred to as the cash surplus or deficit. For purposes of economic analysis, the series is a more complete measure of the impact of Federal financial transactions on the economy than the series on budget receipts and expenditures. Certain Government contractual arrangements, such as the program for lease-purchase of Government buildings, have economic effects which cannot be measured by the payments made in any one period (fig. 12).

CURRENCY, CREDIT, AND SECURITY MARKETS

CURRENCY AND DEPOSITS

During March, demand deposits declined somewhat less than the usual seasonal amount. At the end of the month, total deposits (excluding Government) and currency were 2.7 percent higher than a year earlier.

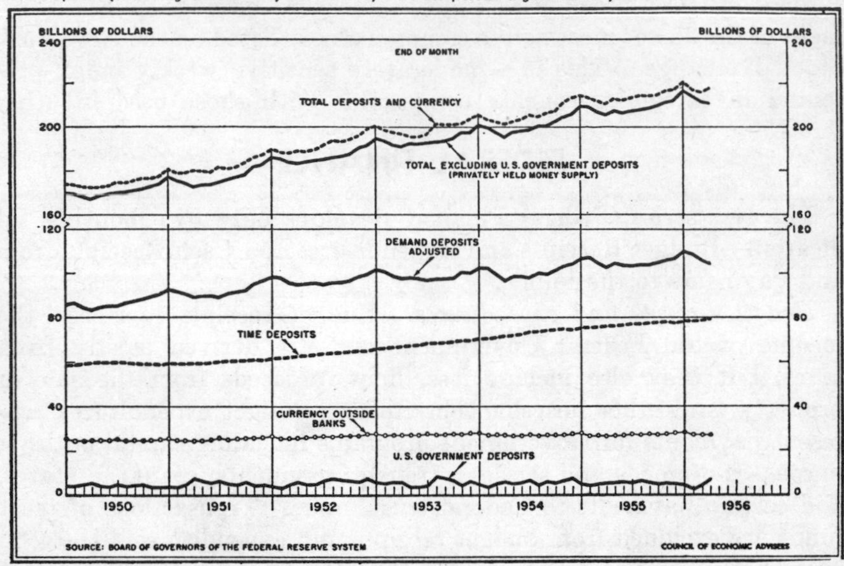

[Billions of dollars]

End of period	Total deposits and currency	U. S. Government deposits [1]	Total excluding U. S. Government deposits (privately held money supply) [2]			
			Total	Currency outside banks	Demand deposits adjusted [3]	Time deposits [4]
1948	172.7	3.6	169.1	26.1	85.5	57.5
1949	173.9	4.1	169.8	25.4	85.8	58.6
1950	180.6	3.7	176.9	25.4	92.3	59.2
1951	189.9	3.9	186.0	26.3	98.2	61.4
1952	200.4	5.6	194.8	27.5	101.5	65.8
1953	205.7	4.8	200.9	28.1	102.5	70.4
1954	214.8	5.1	209.7	27.9	106.6	75.3
1955 [5]	221.0	4.4	216.6	28.3	109.9	78.4
1955: February	212.1	5.1	206.9	26.8	104.5	75.7
March	210.6	5.3	205.3	26.7	102.4	76.2
April	213.0	5.6	207.4	26.7	104.5	76.2
May	212.6	5.9	206.7	26.8	103.3	76.5
June	213.5	5.8	207.7	27.4	103.2	77.1
July	214.6	6.5	208.1	27.1	103.9	77.1
August	214.2	5.6	208.6	27.3	103.9	77.4
September	214.8	5.1	209.7	27.2	104.9	77.7
October	216.7	5.3	211.3	27.3	106.1	77.9
November	217.2	5.0	212.2	27.9	106.9	77.4
December	221.0	4.4	216.6	28.3	109.9	78.4
1956: January [5]	217.2	2.8	214.4	27.1	108.9	78.4
February [5]	216.1	4.5	211.6	27.2	105.6	78.8
March [5]	217.8	7.0	210.8	27.2	104.4	79.3

Source: Economic Indicators, May 1956.

[1] Includes U. S. Government deposits at Federal Reserve banks and commercial and savings banks and U. S. Treasurer's time deposits, open account.

[2] Includes deposits and currency held by State and local governments.

[3] Includes demand deposits, other than interbank and U. S. Government, less cash items in process of collection.

[4] Includes deposits in commercial banks, mutual savings banks, and Postal Savings System, but excludes interbank deposits.

[5] Preliminary estimates.

NOTE.—Detail will not necessarily add to totals because of rounding.

Source: Board of Governors of the Federal Reserve System.

Figure 11.

CASH RECEIPTS FROM AND PAYMENTS TO THE PUBLIC

Federal cash receipts exceeded cash payments by almost $7 billion for the first quarter of 1956, compared with $4.1 billion for the same period last year.

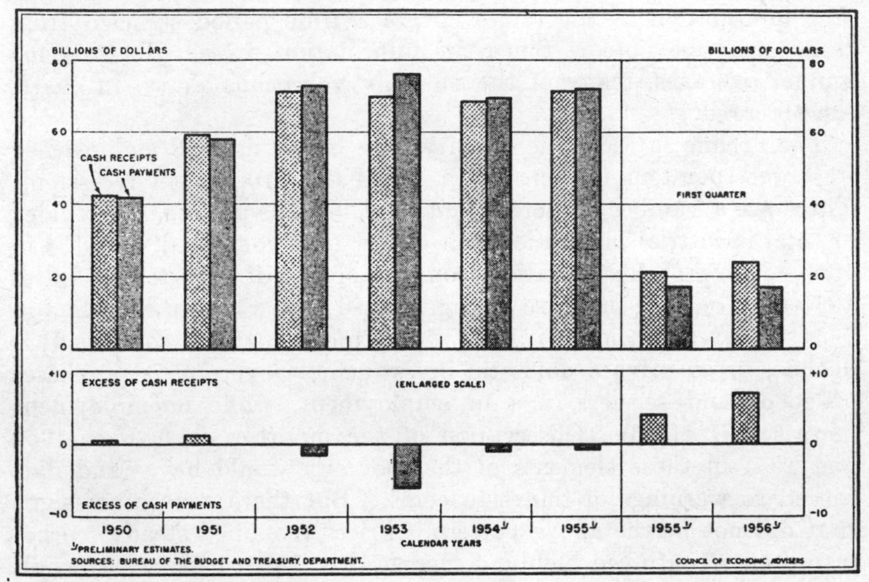

SOURCE: Economic Indicators, May 1956.

Figure 12.

MEANING OF ECONOMIC INDICATORS AS SHOWN IN CONNECTION WITH THE 1954 RECESSION [3]

Some of the data presented in Economic Indicators may be used as thermometers to indicate the status of the economy and to compare it with earlier corresponding periods. Other data may be used as barometers to indicate the possible direction of the economy.

"A great deal of experienced judgment and insight is needed in analyzing and interpreting economic statistics, precisely as in the case of physicians or experts in other fields. It is folly to look for some set of simple curves, or indicators, or multipliers, or to pursue simple analogies with past periods. Recognizing the complexities of the problem claims must be made modestly and above all, the basis of conclusions must be made clear, especially if they are judgments as to the economic outlook based on fragmentary data." [4]

---

[3] This section was prepared by Dr. S. H. McGuire of the Correspondence Branch as one example of analysis of economic data. The period of 1954 was chosen because the changes at that time were most noticeable. The material draws upon the lecture of M. R. Gainsbrugh, previously cited and as indicated, but does not purport to represent his analysis.

[4] Grover W. Ensley, Staff Director, Joint Committee on the Economic Report, United States Congress, "Economic Indicators and Measures of Cyclical Correction," *Social Science*, October 1954, p. 203.

Even in the face of this caution some analysis is undertaken as examples. This limited analysis is based upon the data shown in tables 6 and 7 and in the charts presented in the preceding pages. The information in the tables covers a time period sufficient that trends may be noted. Since the information presented represents annual averages, many of the monthly variations shown in charts are obscured.

The decline in economic activity that began in 1953 and reached its lowest point in 1954 has been called the "10-percent recession." There are a number of factors that revealed this decline. The index of total industrial production was 125 in 1954 compared with 134 in 1953. The monthly variation from the spring of 1953 to the fall of 1954 may be seen in figure 9, page 65. There was also a decline in 1954 in GNP, national income, farm income which continued to decline, gross private domestic investment, Government purchases of goods and services, and in employment, while unemployment increased (table 6). Observation of the monthly changes in 1953 and 1954 in these elements of the economy would have (and did) served as warnings of things to come. But there were other signs that did not fit the above pattern. Prices remained steady; corporate profits continued high and increased in 1955; personal expenditures rose; average weekly hours remained almost steady; and average weekly earnings in manufacturing continued to rise slightly. Consumer credit, and hence buying power, remained high, and consumers showed a willingness to spend. Thus to view these counteracting facts during the period can lead only to a cautious interpretation of the whole. The economy was down, or one might say weak, in spots. On the other hand, these latter facts represented some of the strong and sustaining elements that brought the economy upward in the second half of 1954 and in 1955.

The fact that there were more than 3 million unemployed in 1954 is significant. This number represents about 5 percent of the civilian labor force. It was once assumed that frictional unemployment—those temporarily unemployed while changing jobs and the like—would normally be about 5 percent. Since the war, however, it is believed that unemployment in excess of 3 or 4 percent constitutes an unnecessary waste of manpower. If the 3 to 4 percent estimate of normal frictional unemployment is sound, the 5 percent of 1954 represented a situation of industrial unemployment. In fact, unemployment still stood at 4 percent in 1955 and somewhat higher in the early months of 1956.

Table 6. Summary of Selected Data

	1952	1953	1954	1955	1956 (1st quarter)
Gross national product (billions)	$345. 2	$364. 5	$360. 5	$387. 2	$398. 6
Total national income (billions)	$289. 5	$303. 6	$299. 7	$322. 6	$333. 8
Farm income (billions)	$36. 9	$35. 2	$34. 0	$33. 2	$32. 5
Corporate profit after taxes (billions)	$16. 1	$17. 0	$17. 0	$21. 8	$22. 7
Gross private domestic investment (billions)	$49. 6	$51. 4	$47. 2	$59. 3	$62. 4
Personal expenditures or dispotion of personal income (billions)	$218. 3	$230. 6	$236. 5	$252. 3	$258. 8
Durable goods	$26. 6	$29. 8	$29. 3	$35. 3	$33. 9
Nondurable goods	$116. 0	$118. 9	$120. 9	$125. 9	$129. 9
Services	$75. 7	$81. 8	$86. 4	$91. 2	$95. 1
Government purchases—goods and services (billions)	$77. 5	$84. 5	$77. 0	$75. 9	$77. 4
Employment (thousands)	61. 293	62. 213	61. 238	63. 193	62. 848
Unemployment (thousands) [a]	1. 673	1. 602	3. 230	2. 654	2. 877
Average weekly hours (mfg.)	40. 7	40. 5	39. 7	40. 7	40. 5
Average weekly earnings (mfg.)	$67. 97	$71. 69	$71. 86	$76. 52	$78. 50
Total industrial production index [b]	124	134	125	139	143
New construction (billions)	$33. 0	$35. 3	$37. 6	$42. 2	$41. 5
Prices—consumer index [b]	113. 5	114. 4	114. 8	114. 5	114. 6
Prices—wholesale [b]	111. 6	110. 1	110. 3	110. 7	112. 4
Consumer credit—total (billions)	$25. 827	$29. 537	$30. 125	$36. 225	$35. 469

SOURCE: From *Economic Indicators,* May 1956 (selected).

[a] Percent of civilian labor force unemployed, 2.7, 2.5, 5.0, 4.0, and 4.4.

[b] 1947–49 equals 100.

In addition to the status of employment and unemployment, the above data reveal only two items pointing to weakness in the economy in 1955 and first quarter of 1956. The most important of these is the decline in farm income that has continued since 1952. This, of course, must have its effects upon other sectors of the economy. Government spending or purchase of goods and services was less in 1954 than in 1953 and has continued somewhat lower than in 1953 (fig. 6, page 52). This reduction, however, is minor, about 2 percent of the gross national product.

On the other hand, the strong sectors in 1955 and 1956 are the gross national product, the national income, corporate profits, gross private domestic investment, personal expenditures for durable and nondurable goods and services, and average weekly earnings. Consumers still have money and credit with which to buy, and the Survey Research Center of the University of Michigan reports that the "predominant expectation among consumers is that prosperity will continue." It adds that consumers are not as optimistic now as they were a year ago.

The total picture of the economy cannot be constructed from the above data alone. The index of "total industrial production" represents only about one-fourth of the total. The status of inventories is not shown, and that is important. The slack in automobile production does not appear, nor does the amount of new housing nor the rental demand for houses. In table 7 may be seen the continued improvement of production since 1954 in the following selected sectors of both durable and nondurable manufactures: primary metals, fabricated metal products, machinery, transportation equipment, lumber and products, textiles and apparel, paper and printing, chemical and petroleum products, foods, beverages and tobacco, and consumer durable goods. In all of these the index of production has continued to rise, with very minor exceptions for certain months, since 1954. In this table also may be seen the weak spots that were apparent among these industries during the recession. The only ones that did not feel the effect of or contribute to the "10-percent recession" were paper and printing, chemical and petroleum products, and foods, beverages and tobacco. Note that the others, under durable manufacturers, are basic since each of them is a contributor to other end products among durable goods and not itself primarily an end product.

An analysis of economic data can be meaningful only when the economy is examined as a whole insofar as the information permits. An isolated fact may be insignificant but when seen in relation to other facts it may be revealing. It would be hazardous to make any predictions on the basis of the above data. However, certain favorable elements are discernible. The GNP and the national income are high and appear to be moving upward; in the same class are corporate profits and gross private domestic investments. Personal consumer expenditures, average weekly earnings, and consumer credit would suggest that the public has the means of purchasing a tremendous output of goods and services. A pessimist, however, might inquire if consumer credit is too high. Are we about to reach the point where payments will have to catch up with purchases? Industrial production and new construction appear favorable on the whole. Prices have remained steady even through the recession, and this would seem to be in harmony with continued high profits and, hence, high productivity to reap the profits. On the other hand, farm income continues to be discouraging; unemployment has continued to plague the economy for more than 2 years. Federal, State, and local taxes continue to take a large portion of the national income.

During 1952 to 1954 annual cash payments by the Federal Government have exceeded its cash receipts from the public. But in the first quarter of 1956 the Government received from the public nearly $7 billion more than it paid out to the public. Would this change, if continued, stimulate business or would it reduce the buying power of the public and tend to be deflationary? (Fig. 12, page 73 and tables 8 and 9, pages 90–91.) What are the meaning and effect of the continued increase in the amount of total deposits and currency? (Fig. 11, page 72.) What is the effect of the United States balance of payments position in foreign trade? Our total exports continue to increase and to remain above rising imports.

The above facts and the suggested questions must all be considered in any analysis of the trend of the economy.

Table 7. Index of Production—Selected Manufactures

	1952	1953	1954	1955	1956 (1st quarter)
Durable manufactures:					
Primary metals	116	132	108	140	147
Fabricated metal products	121	136	123	134	134
Machinery	147	160	142	155	163
Transportation equipment	154	189	175	203	201
Lumber and products	111	118	115	127	124
Nondurable manufactures:					
Textiles and apparel	105	107	100	109	110
Paper and printing	118	125	125	137	140
Chemical and petroleum products	133	142	142	159	166
Foods, beverages, and tobacco	106	107	106	109	111
Consumer durable goods	105	127	116	147	138

X
WAGE LEVELS AND LABOR UNIONS

THE DETERMINATION OF WAGE RATES

All production is brought about by some combination of the factors of production—land, labor, and capital. There are many combinations of the three factors, however, and the productiveness of labor itself is, in turn, dependent on the effectiveness of these combinations. Thus productivity of labor is affected by the amount of land and capital used, the efficiency with which the three factors support each other, and the skill of management in coordinating the factors of production.

By and large, wage rates are fixed under the law of supply and demand, as are other prices. Current writing tends to stress wage problems, and it is not uncommon to find economics texts without direct reference to wage theory. This is a regrettable omission, for while there are innumerable interferences with the law of supply and demand in the everyday industrial picture, in the long run, the law does apply to wages.

Marginal productivity. The marginal productivity theory of wages assumes that each worker's wage will be an amount equal to the marginal product of his labor within his own labor group. To determine the loss of production which results from the withdrawal of one worker from a particular phase of production is to determine that worker's marginal contribution. The worth of the individual's labor then is reflected in the sales of the company's product. Further, this theory assumes the payment of this marginal wage as almost automatic. If employment conditions are reasonably good, no worker need take less than his marginal wage and no employer need pay any more.

There are many weaknesses in the marginal productivity theory of wage determination. It assumes full employment and the complete mobility of labor; it supposes that labor can move to other employment opportunities and is willing to do so. It overlooks the lack of mobility in many workers, the accumulation of seniority and pension rights with the current employer, and loyalty to a product. It does not take into consideration the mechanics of wage bargaining between unions and corporations. Today's mass production methods and the general complexity of current production processes, make it extremely difficult to determine the marginal product of any individual. Labor union contracts are for relatively brief periods of time and actually do reflect short-run conditions such as variations in the business cycle, monopolistic labor union practices, and the imperfect mobility of labor. In the long run, however, economists feel that wage rates do reflect marginal productivity and that wages tend to approach equilibrium. Several recent studies have confirmed earlier ones that the current proportion of industrial earnings going to labor are very close to the general proportion maintained since 1900, through good times and bad. The marginal productivity theory of wage determination is still valuable as a base for consideration of wage problems.

COMPETING LABOR GROUPS

An individual looking for employment may feel that he is in competition with every other unemployed person. This is not generally true. He is competing mainly with those who enjoy the same skills that he does. Of course under certain conditions, such as advancing age, an individual may have to drop down to a lower wage class, which becomes his new level. Generally the wage groups may be listed as unskilled, semiskilled, skilled, clerical, executive and professional. There are also special groups of highly talented, and highly paid persons such as artists, actors, athletes, and athletic coaches, whose working life is often rather short. While we think of these persons as highly paid, they may be actually underpaid. It is said that Babe Ruth had to be content with a salary of $80,000 because the Yankee baseball park was the only one large enough to hold enough customers to make this salary possible. No other club could offer more.

Some jobs are more desirable than others and the choice is often reflected in the wage rate. White collar workers may get less per hour but are assured of greater regularity of employment. A university professor has a long period of preparation, but his prestige is high. The glamour of public office may offset its low pay.

THE CHANGING SUPPLY OF LABOR

It is becoming more and more common for women, single and married, to work for wages steadily or for considerable periods of time. The amount of new labor coming into the labor force each year depends in part on the number of years of schooling that are customary, minimum age regulations for employment, and the like. Higher wages may bring workers into industry more quickly. As demand increases, older workers are called back into the labor market. In America the number of workers available is often as important as their skills. Engineers use machines to break down manufacturing processes in order to bring them within the performance limits of the skills available.

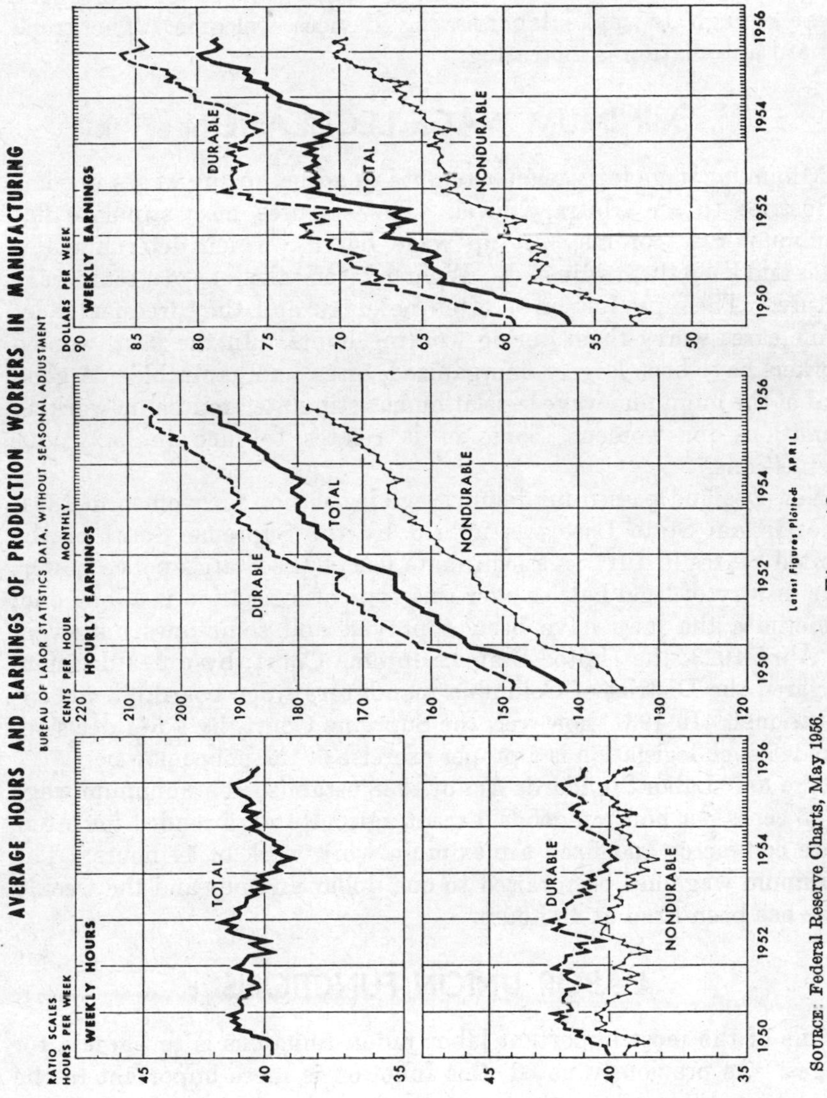

SOURCE: Federal Reserve Charts, May 1956.

Figure 13.

Labor has historically been in short supply in the United States and has tended to be relatively highly paid. Machines which save labor have been generally welcomed in America except for fairly brief periods when business was at a low level. These machines have increased productivity and wages. Currently the labor shortage is great enough to make labor-saving devices welcome. The trend toward automation is increasing.

MINIMUM WAGE LEGISLATION

Minimum wage legislation attempts to adjust or lift wages in some industries to an arbitrary level. The statutes may stipulate flat minimum rates or may set up wage boards, which determine fair rates and keep them adjusted. Women often take jobs of a temporary nature. Their production is often not high and they frequently let home cares worry them during working hours. In the past, women workers have been largely unorganized, often unorganizable. A good deal of the minimum wage legislation has stipulated minimum working conditions for women. Some of it relates to men in hazardous occupations.

New Zealand passed minimum wage legislation for women in 1894. The Oregon State Law was upheld by the Supreme Court of the United States in 1917 as a legitimate use of the State's police power. The history of legal battles over this type of legislation is a long one; sometimes the laws have been approved and sometimes outlawed. In April 1923, the United States Supreme Court, by a 5–3 decision, declared the District of Columbia mandatory wage board law unconstitutional. In 1937, however, the Supreme Court, by a 5–4 decision, decided such legislation is a proper exercise of the police power.

The Fair Labor Standards Act of 1938 established a minimum wage of 25 cents per hour on goods, except agricultural, intended for interstate commerce and fixed a maximum work week of 44 hours. The minimum wage has been raised to one dollar an hour and the weekly base has been fixed at 40 hours.

LABOR UNION FUNCTIONS

One of the most important labor union functions is to bargain for wages. As previously noted, this function is more important in the short term than it is in the long run. Another labor union function is to seek favoring legislation, perhaps more important a few years ago than now. They also furnish protection, support, and services to the individual workers. As machines and factories grow more automatic and firms constantly become larger, the individual worker may develop a feeling of frustration. He wants to be proud of his product and of his company but is apt to feel that the company cares little whether he appears for work or is replaced by another worker or even by a robot. It is the function of the union to provide the concern for the plight of the worker which the individual employer once gave, but which the corporation may fail to bestow.

The more keen the competition, the more precarious is the position of the older worker. Medical science is helping the men and women to live longer and to remain efficient. Seniority rights and pension buildups daily become of more importance to more persons. Protection of the seniority rights of older workers against the pressure of younger workers has become one of the most important duties of the modern labor union. Unions also collect funds with which to carry out their programs and, of course, call concerted work stoppages or strikes.

Wage bargaining. Labor is not a commodity, says labor itself, and so does the Clayton Act. In the broader sense, of course, it is similar to a commodity; it is a labor service to the producer that the laborer has to offer, to sell.

In earlier days spokesmen for management were wont to say that they did not like unions for very many reasons, that they were unnecessary, and that they preferred to deal with an applicant for a job, "man to man." Labor spokesmen contend the employment representative really speaks for management and represents the collective size and importance of that plant. As such there is no meeting of the minds, no give and take, no man to man discussion. There is merely a corporate offer on the part of management which the individual worker can accept or refuse. His ability to refuse will depend on his personal necessities. Says the union, allow us to send a representative of the collective labor within a plant to talk with the management representative of the entire plant and then we can really bargain, group to group, the representative of labor and the representative of management.

The student of industrial ethics has long since convinced himself that, under the natural law, every worker has a right to a living wage in return for useful labor, as long as the earth remains capable of ministering to the needs of all its inhabitants. Further, says the industrial ethicist, man has not only a right to a living wage but a right to a "just" wage, if it is greater than a living wage. He is entitled to the marginal product of his labor.

Strikes. How does labor compel the employer to respect the rights to which it feels entitled? The ultimate answer seems to be resort to a concerted labor stoppage, a strike. The same industrial ethicists have declared that a strike can be regarded as just only where there is a serious difficulty and when all other means of solution have been tried and have failed. The United States Supreme Court, under Chief Justice Taft's leadership, long ago declared that since an individual has a right to quit his job singly, he must have the right to do so collectively. Actually the worker on strike wants his job back and does not wish it filled by another. Picketing and boycotting are limited by many court decisions.

In 1937 the Supreme Court in a Labor Board case seemed to declare the sitdown strike an illegal interference with the property rights of private owners. A concerted sitdown strike by large numbers of workers does not lend itself to quick and legal settlement. Many students of labor problems feel that the great mass production industries could not have been unionized in 1937 without the use of the sitdown strike. Now that these unions are established, a concerted work stoppage, without the sitdown or sit-in feature, is all that is required to force a solution to the existing dispute.

TYPES OF LABOR UNIONS

There are two main kinds of unions in the United States, the craft union and the industrial union. The craft union represents a personal skill peculiar to the worker, and the union bands together all possessors of that skill without regard to the place of employment. The industrial union bands together all the employees of a firm, or of an industry, and assigns appropriate group wage rates to relative skills.

The American Federation of Labor (AFL) appeared in 1881 and assumed that name in 1886. It is a federation of independent craft unions, loosely combined into a protective association. This craft type of federation succeeded the Knights of Labor which had been formed in 1869. The Knights of Labor invited to membership all who were interested in the problems of labor. They attracted a considerable professional following and eventually exhibited political tendencies. The AFL likewise showed a general labor interest, but its organization was based only on the craft.

In 1935 a group within the AFL formed the "Committee for Industrial Organization" with the avowed intention of unionizing the great mass production industries and bringing them within the Federation. While District 50 of the United Mine Workers, then part of the AFL, always permitted the formation of an industrial union, it was used largely by the miners and there was little enthusiasm within the rank and file of the Federation for this type of union.

The management of the mass production industries could demonstrate that their wage rates were at least equal to those of any other employer and were often far higher. Some individual owners, such as Henry Ford, were bitterly opposed to union interference with the prerogatives of management. It took the sitdown strike technique to accomplish the task.

In November 1938, the Committee for Industrial Organization decided to be independent of the American Federation of Labor and took the name of the "Congress of Industrial Organizations" (CIO). Since that time there has been some withdrawal from the CIO on the part of more independently minded unions, and in 1956 the AFL and the more conservatively minded CIO groups were reamalgamated as the AFL–CIO.

XI
PUBLIC FINANCE AND REVENUES

NATURE OF PUBLIC FINANCE

Since 1900 the role of Government in the organization and functioning of all modern societies has increased several fold. Government today is big business, perhaps our largest "industry."

Total Federal, State, and local expenditures in the United States absorbed only 7 percent of the national income in 1890. In 1940, these expenditures took about 22 percent of the national income; in 1944, about 55 percent; in 1948, approximately 24 percent; and during the Korean war, almost one-third. Social-welfare outlays alone are reported to take about 20 percent of the British national income and all Government expenditures, about 40 percent.

In addition to such regulating activities as those carried on by the Civil Aeronautics Board, the Interstate Commerce Commission, the Federal Trade Commission, and the Antitrust Division of the U. S. Department of Justice, the Federal Government operates numerous enterprises including the Post Office, the Tennessee Valley Authority, and the Atomic Energy Commission. Many municipalities operate one or more local utilities. Social-welfare activities and programs are very large in all Government sectors.

The Government buys defense products and builds schools and roads. The manufacture of most defense products and most construction activities, however, are carried on by private business. The Government is the purchaser but not the producer. In any case activities of this nature performed by or for the Government require large public revenues.

THE LAW AND ECONOMIC ACTIVITY

The protection of the public safety, health, morals, and welfare have long been recognized as legitimate purposes on the part of Government. They justify interference with business and its regulation.

The power to tax is used by Government to "regulate" economic activity as well as to raise revenues. From the earliest days, the United States courts have sustained taxes imposed with the collateral intent to bring about control. In 1819 the Supreme Court held in *McCulloch* vs. *Maryland*, that the power to tax is the power to destroy. Although the primary purpose of the income tax is to raise revenue, it can be used in some degree to distribute wealth. Other control types of taxes are intercorporate dividend taxes, inheritance taxes, taxes on imported goods, and graduated taxes on chain stores which increase with the number of units.

TAX SYSTEMS

Governments raise money in four ways—by taxes, by borrowing, by printing paper money, and by operating public businesses at a profit. Tobacco, salt, coffee, and gambling monopolies yield revenues to many European governments. American municipalities depend on earnings from operating liquor stores and electric power and gas plants for a portion of their revenues.

In the 19th century, the American individual States and municipalities relied mainly for revenues on the general property tax, a tax on real estate and on personal property. Up to 1860 the Federal Government relied chiefly on customs receipts; liquor and tobacco excises were added after the war. By 1909 a Federal corporation tax of 1 percent had been imposed. The 16th Amendment to the Constitution cleared the way for a personal income tax system in 1913. Currently most states also impose income taxes, as do some cities including St. Louis and Philadelphia. Federal inheritance taxes were imposed in 1916, and many excise and customs taxes have since been added.

State governments no longer depend on real property taxes. The leading sources of State taxes are the gasoline tax, the general sales tax, and a payroll tax for unemployment insurance. Liquor and tobacco taxes are important revenue sources to the States, as is the license fee for operating motor vehicles. Local governments continue to rely on the general property tax but have quite generally added excise and sales taxes.

FEDERAL, STATE, AND LOCAL EXPENDITURES

Villages, towns, and cities are creatures of the several States. The service functions of government such as local roads, schools, and social welfare have been traditionally assigned to them. But there have long been instances of the inability of these localities to carry the load. The States have long since helped the localities by taking over some functions, by allocating additional tax sources to them, by sharing State tax revenues, and by grants-in-aid.

During the depression of the 1930's the States themselves faltered fiscally. The Federal Government set up approximately 40 grants-in-aid programs to assist them. They include old-age assistance, unemployment compensation, dependent children programs, and the construction of highways and hospitals.

PRINCIPLES OF TAXATION

Modern economic writing lays less stress on the matter of equity or justice as a principle in taxation. Before income taxes were as widespread as at present, taxes were often placed on various types of business activities and products. Business promptly shifted the taxes forward whenever possible. This tendency is recognized today and is taken into consideration when a tax is imposed.

In earlier times there was much outcry over the idea of sales taxes. It was argued that the same sales tax on the loaf of bread of a poor man was a serious matter to him and of no importance to those better off. Earlier forms of sales taxes exempted food and work-type clothing from taxation. As the needs of Government increased with city living and with higher concepts of acceptable welfare services, sales taxes increased in general use and have been gradually imposed on most retail sales. They do raise money; perhaps the generally prevailing standard of living in the United States has overridden the earlier equity considerations. Income taxes are collected at rather low wage and salary levels also but in some countries are so progressive as to discourage further effort to earn.

In any consideration of taxation principles, the *ability-to-pay* theory is widely discussed. Taxes should be progressive, according to this principle; people with higher incomes have the capacity to pay a larger percentage of their incomes as taxes than do those of lower incomes. However, views as to the proper levels at which to place progressive income, estate, and inheritance taxes vary directly with the political, social, and economic convictions of those taking part in the discussion. There seems to be no sound, scientific way by which we can determine proper or correct tax levels on an ability-to-pay theory.

The *benefit* principle is popular in tax theory. Taxes should be imposed in proportion to the benefits expected from the expenditures. Examples of special assessments are those on property so located that it benefits directly from the improvement, such as sewers and water mains. Gasoline taxes finance road building, and payroll taxes finance old-age pensions. This principle cannot be applied in all areas of government benefits, but it does have many special applications, such as the uses indicated, and is a major consideration in fixing fees charged by government units.

The *equality of opportunity* theory or principle would use taxation to promote such opportunity. The use of the tax system to bring about an equality of wealth and income may succeed in that accomplishment, but it may also limit opportunity. Highly progressive forms of taxation can prevent the accumulation of wealth by persons of ability and thus prevent them from challenging the position of those already possessing wealth and income. Such a tax system would stratify society and impede class mobility.

In general, taxes should be productive, readily understandable by the taxpayer, low in collection costs, minimize taxpayer annoyance and difficult to evade.

Table 8.—Federal, State, and Local Tax Revenues, by Sources, Fiscal Year 1953 [a]

Tax	Amount (millions of dollars)				Distribution among governments (percentages)			
	All governments	Federal	State	Local [b]	All governments	Federal	State	Local [b]
Net income:								
Individual	30, 838	29, 784	969	85	100. 0	96. 6	3. 1	0. 3
Corporate	22, 057	21, 239	810	8	100. 0	96. 3	3. 7	(c)
Inheritance, estate, and gift	1, 106	881	222	3	100. 0	79. 7	20. 1	3
Tobacco	[d] 2, 119	1, 652	467	(e)	100. 0	78. 0	22. 0	(e)
Alcoholic beverages	[d] 3, 268	[f] 2, 723	[f] 545	(e)	100. 0	83. 3	16. 7	(e)
Gasoline	[d] 2, 908	891	2, 017	(e)	100. 0	30. 6	69. 4	(e)
Amusements	[d] 434	[g] 416	[h] 18	(e)	100. 0	95. 9	4. 1	(e)
Other selective excises	5, 887	[i] 4, 825	804	258	100. 0	82. 0	13. 7	4. 4
General sales	2, 802		2, 433	369	100. 0		86. 8	13. 2
Property	8, 647		365	8, 282	100. 0		4. 2	95. 8
Other	2, 353		1, 892	461	100. 0		80. 4	19. 6
Total	82, 419	62, 411	10, 542	9, 466	100. 0	75. 7	12. 8	11. 5

SOURCE: Lecture, ICAF, A. G. Buehler, 2 September 1955.

[a] Exclusive of social insurance contributions. Tax collections include penalties and interest but are net of refunds which are substantial in amount in the case of Federal income taxes and State gasoline taxes.

[b] Local tax revenues for fiscal year 1952. Includes collections for Washington, D. C.

[c] Less than .05 percent.

[d] Exclusive of local governments.

[e] Distribution not available; amounts included in "Other selective excises."

[f] Includes, in addition to excises, Federal occupational or special taxes amounting to 21.5 million dollars and State licenses amounting to 79 million dollars.

[g] Includes taxes on admissions to theaters, concerts, cabarets, etc., club dues and initiation fees, bowling alleys, pool tables, and coin-operated devices.

[h] Includes both excises and licenses but does not include amounts collected from admission by the 17 States which tax admissions under the general sales tax.

[i] Includes customs duties which amount to 596 million dollars.

Treasury Department, Analysis Staff, Tax Division, 1954.

SOURCE: Federal: "Review of the 1954 Budget," 27 August 1953; "Treasury Bulletin," December 1953. Data on internal revenue refunds from tabulations to be published in "Annual Report of the Commissioner of Internal Revenue" for fiscal year 1953; data on customs refunds from tabulations to be published in "Annual Report of the Secretary of the Treasury" for fiscal year 1953. State: Bureau of the Census, "State Tax Collections in 1953," 31 August 1953. Local: Bureau of the Census, "Summary of Governmental Finances in 1952," 2 November 1953.

Table 9. Expenditures of Federal, State, and Local Governments [a]
(Millions)
Selected fiscal years 1890–1954

Year	Total	Federal [b]	State [c]	Local [d]
1915	$2, 616	$746	$485	[e] $1, 385
1919	21, 150	18, 448	692	2, 010
1923	8, 058	3, 137	1, 320	3, 601
1927	10, 156	2, 837	1, 859	5, 460
1932	12, 751	4, 659	2, 506	5, 586
1937	16, 051	7, 756	3, 134	5, 161
1938	15, 539	6, 877	3, 409	5, 253
1939	17, 712	8, 978	3, 591	5, 143
1940	17, 674	9, 205	3, 565	4, 904
1941	21, 774	13, 465	3, 542	4, 767
1942	43, 805	34, 291	4, 485	5, 029
1944	104, 245	95, 378	4, 180	4, 687
1946	74, 093	60, 937	6, 202	6, 954
1948	53, 925	33, 898	9, 441	10, 586
1950	67, 677	40, 824	12, 659	14, 194
1951	72, 522	45, 981	12, 512	14, 029
1952	96, 209	67, 892	13, 349	14, 968
1953	107, 617	77, 529	14, 089	15, 999
1954	103, 247	71, 547	[f] 14, 700	17, 000

SOURCE: Department of Commerce, Treasury Department, and Tax Foundation.

[a] Exclusive of debt retirement; grants-in-aid are counted as expenditures of the first disbursing unit. State and local data for 1942–1953 not strictly comparable with earlier years due to changes in reporting.

[b] "Net budget expenditures" plus benefit payments and administrative expenses of the Old-Age and Survivors' Insurance Trust Fund and the Railroad Retirement Account and benefit payments of the Railroad Unemployment Insurance Account.

[c] "Total Expenditure" (excluding debt retirement) less aid received from other governments.

[d] "Total Expenditure" (excluding debt retirement) less aid received from other governments. Data for years other than 1915, 1932, 1952, and 1953 are Tax Foundation estimates.

[e] 1913 amount; 1915 available.

[f] Estimated by Tax Foundation.

PUBLIC REVENUES

Taxes furnish the greatest part of all public revenues. Funds derived from public loans are really borrowed purchasing power obtained in anticipation of later tax revenues. To the extent that government borrowing exceeds revenues, except in anticipation thereof, there is, of course, the creation of money. This situation will have an effect on the purchasing power of the dollar. Revenues from the public domain are largely a matter of history. The Post Office is regarded as a public service. Operations carried on by the Tennessee Valley Authority for private users are intended only to return their costs. There is no intention to charge rates that will result in any considerable profit.

Considerable discussion has taken place over proper bookkeeping methods for Government enterprises. If the costs and revenues of a commercial-type operation are carried as merely parts of the general budget activities of the Government agency supervising the venture, there is less notice taken by the public of the ultimate cost to the taxpayer or of revenues from the enterprise. It is argued by many that the accounts of Government enterprises should be listed separately to determine whether they are a tax burden or yield a profit. On the other hand it is contended that Government enterprises do not seek profits as such and that the accounting method makes little difference.

XII
INTERNATIONAL ECONOMICS AND WORLD TRADE

REASONS FOR INTERNATIONAL TRADE

Perhaps the basic reason for international trade is still the division of labor plus the unequal distribution of natural resources. Long before the Industrial Revolution, world trade consisted largely of the exchange of natural products among the producing areas of the earth; grapes from France, coffee from Turkey, cotton from Egpyt, and wool from England were among the well-known articles of commerce.

As the Industrial Revolution in England got well under way, Britain became the workshop of the world and busily traded manufactured goods for foodstuffs and for more raw materials out of which to fabricate still more manufactured goods. The Industrial Revolution eventually spread to the Continent, and a new rush for colonies began. These colonies were not only sources of raw materials but, to a limited extent, provided a market for finished goods.

To the earliest writers on international trade, it seemed almost the intent of a benevolent Providence that certain areas should produce things so nicely interchangeable with other areas. As the industrial era lengthened, writers stressed the regional nature of foreign trade. Certain regions seem to supplement naturally the production of other nearby regions and were natural traders with each other. If the region happened to encompass two or more nationalities, the trade of the area became international trade.

It may be said, as an aside, that after the acquisition of satellites, Russia arbitrarily assigned them production tasks quite foreign to what they had previously performed. This destroyed much of the formerly existing interregional trade and forced new trade alignments inside and outside the iron curtain. It remains to be seen how long these new arrangements will continue.

Today's world trade accomplishes many purposes. It often serves to eliminate surpluses, such as those of wheat, cotton, tobacco, and pork. It provides resources not available at home—coffee, tea, rubber, tin, the newer metals, and some types of sugar. Foreign trade is likewise due to specialization. England's climate continues to give English worsteds an unchallenged superiority; Swedish steel is superb in quality while that of the United States excels in quantity and is lower in price; cheap labor formerly gave the Chinese the edge in the business of making women's hairnets.

IMPORTANCE OF INTERNATIONAL TRADE

International trade is of much greater consequence than the overall statistics would suggest. Since World War II the foreign trade of the United States has averaged only 6 or 7 percent of our total trade, but the importance of this trade is not thus measured. In many industries, in many raw materials, and in foodstuffs, the export percentage of production reaches 20 to 30 percent of the total. Examples include raw cotton and leaf tobacco, lubricating oil, sewing machines, and various types of industrial machines. These industries would be in real trouble without international trade, and so would many subsidiary industries which rely on the export of these goods. The railroads are accustomed to deliver export products in these proportions to the ports, and the ports have been built up to handle the volume. Both would feel any decrease in foreign trade (fig. 14).

IMPEDIMENTS TO TRADE

The question of tariffs *vs.* free trade is almost a matter of emotion The older economists well-nigh in total, and many yet today, are convinced that any barrier to foreign trade is an interference with the division of labor and therefore contrary to all commonsense. They see slight virtue in only one of the arguments in favor of tariffs, that of the "infant industry." There are some areas of the world that are natural to certain kinds of production, given a resident population to be served by that industry. An example is Pittsburgh which, with nearby coal and easy access to iron ore and limestone, is a natural steel center. Free traders say the industry would eventually grow up there without protection. They will admit that the timing of the industry's appearance might be hurried by protecting the infant steel production but always add that no one ever heard of an infant industry growing up and asking for relief from further protection. Currently there are several industries in the United States that would like nothing better than to see the freeing of world trade from all protection. The infants have finally become sturdy adults.

There are many arguments offered by those who seek the protection of tariffs and other devices to encourage manufacturing in nonindustrialized areas. It must be admitted that most of these claims are not valid. However, there is always the open question whether the organized industries in older areas will show enough vitality to satisfy the growing needs of nonindustrialized areas.

Colonial trade. The race to acquire colonies resulted in several varieties of colonialism. As the developers and managers went out to live in the colonies in order to bring out the raw materials, their descendants came to regard themselves as native residents of the area. As the colonies grew and prospered, the mother areas grew and prospered also, and it became more and more common to invest in the colonies, developing them even further. Trade tended to follow the flag. Some countries followed a "closed door" and others an "open door" policy as to development of the colonies by other than their own nationals.

The next step for the colonies, naturally, was to manufacture at least the cheaper grades of goods at the site of the raw materials. The colonial industries demanded protection. The position of the English dominions was for a long time contrary to that of England, who wanted no interference with trade. As the dominions grew in size and importance, they eventually worked out a dominion trading system wherein the group members gave preference to each other at the expense of all traders outside the group. Today England is quite glad to enjoy this preference. The dominion preferential trading system was, in many ways, a manifestation of anticolonialism but on the part of Englishmen themselves living permanently with their descendants in areas other than the United Kingdom. The dominion system knitted them tightly together.

A second kind of anticolonialism is now being manifested by the inhabitants of colonial areas. They prefer outright freedom from foreign influence. The problem is not yet solved politically, but these areas are intent on developing their own manufacturing facilities. The foreign investor, however, is not as content to lend his money as formerly. Current rates of profit are much less, investments are not recovered as quickly, and there is more danger of confiscation or nationalization of plants, especially in time of depression.

International cartels. Industries often try to protect themselves privately, and without regard for national borders, by establishing *cartels.* Cartels, national or international, may consist of agreements within an industry as to common action on many points such as pricing, markups, and the division of territory for production or sales purposes. Cartels were once strong in Germany, are encouraged in England currently, and are legal in several countries on the Continent. The United States has discouraged them in Europe since the close of World War II, but the European Iron and Steel Community is permitted the use of all self-protective devices. Cartels are, of course, illegal in the United States, although industry understandings sometimes exist.

International commodity agreements. International agreements for the production, distribution, and price stabilization of foodstuffs and raw materials are known as commodity agreements. They are participated in to a limited extent by the United States and are often

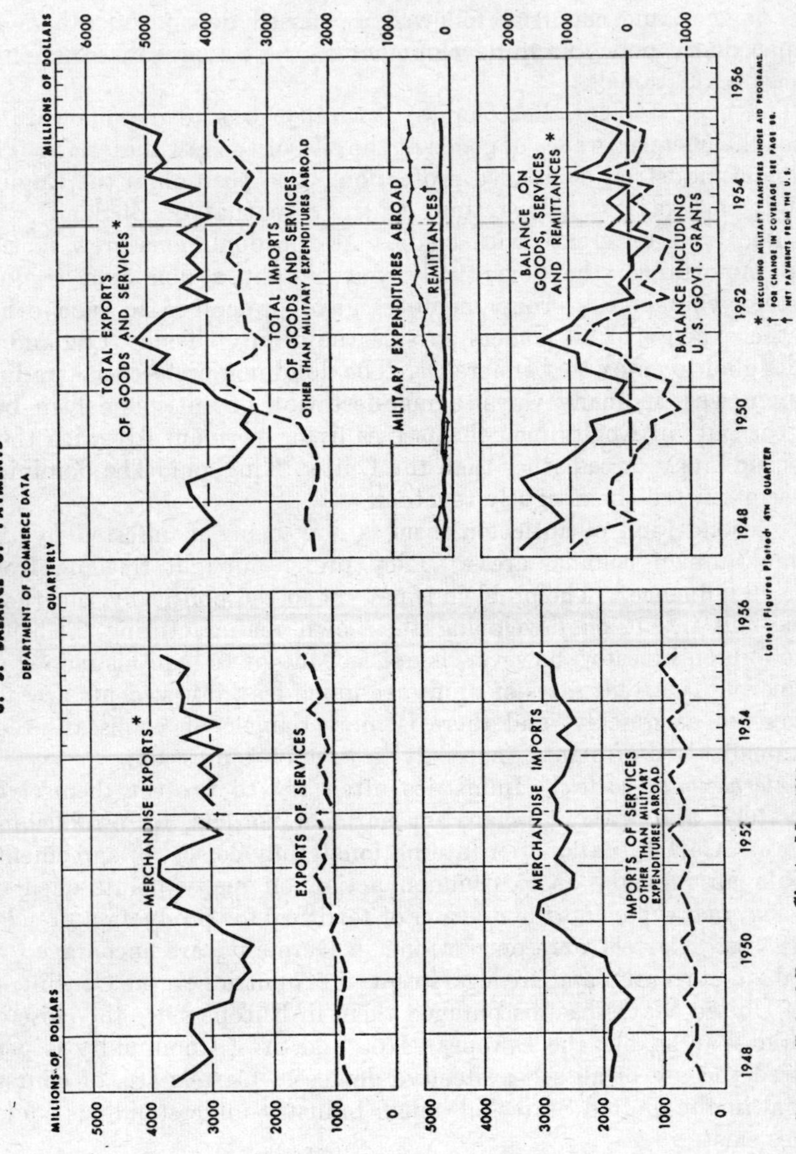

SOURCE: Federal Reserve Charts, May 1956.

Figure 14.

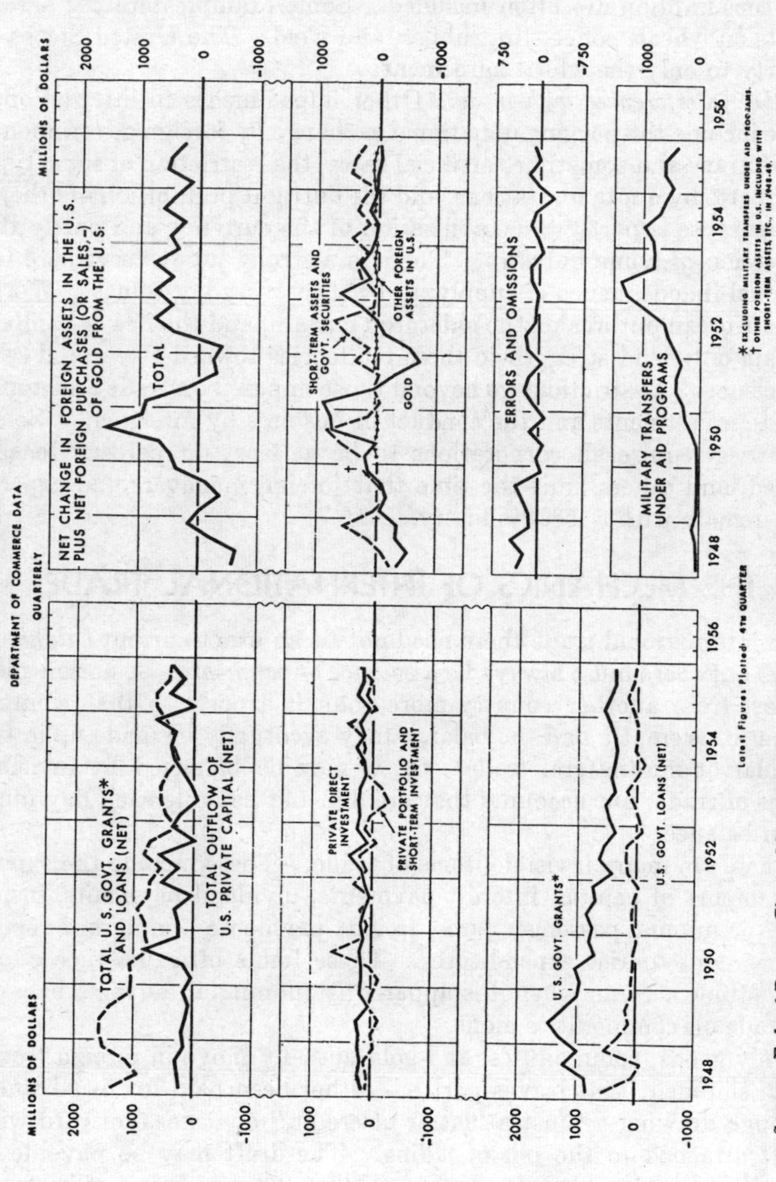

SOURCE: Federal Reserve Charts, May 1956.

Figure 14—Continued

arranged between governments, which are required to take the consumer interest into consideration as well as the interest of the producer. A floor price as well as a ceiling price is usual, and quotas for production and consumption are often included. Some examples are the agreements on wheat, coffee, tin, rubber, and wool. The United States is a party to only the wheat agreement.

Other interferences with trade. Other impediments to international trade include the pegging of national exchange by foreign governments at arbitrary and sometimes artificial rates, the restriction of some type of imports by quota limitations, and the outright prohibition of others. The purpose is partly the stabilization of the currency and partly the protection of home industry. There is a strong urge everywhere for national independence of supply, at least in everyday things. World wars, Korean outbreaks, the older iron curtain, and the newer bamboo curtain only lend strength to these tendencies toward attempted self-sufficiency. Restrictions go beyond those imposed on trade and apply also to investments and the conduct of business by foreigners. Some countries require all corporations to be at least 60 percent locally owned, and others limit the time that foreign managers and experts may remain with a local industry.

THE MECHANICS OF INTERNATIONAL TRADE

In international trade there need not be an exact current *balance of trade*, but there must always be a *balance of payments*. A nation may import from another country more than it exports to that country rather consistently and the balance may eventually be made up in triangular or multilateral trade. Or, it may be balanced by invisible items of trade, but accounts that are due and payable each day must be in balance.

There are many invisible items of trade. These include the export and import of capital, interest payments, dividend payments, insurance premiums, passenger fares, freight payments, immigrant remittances, and tourist expenditures. These items often balance a nation's trade account when it is apparently running an adverse balance of trade on commodities alone.

Only goods, commodities, and gold actually move in foreign trade. Each shipment that leaves port has either been paid for in advance, through drawing against a "letter of credit," or it goes forward with draft attached to the bill of lading. The draft may be payable at sight but is more likely to be payable at the expiration of a stated period of time, perhaps 180 days. When the draft arrives on the other side, the bank that receives it requires the importer to make satisfactory arrangements for payment on the date when the draft becomes due and then releases the bill of lading to him. Only when he is in possession of the duplicate bill of lading, can the importer get delivery of the foreign shipment. Drafts become due and payable every day and must be paid or dishonored. If necessary, gold must be shipped to complete the payment.

In time of war or emergency it often becomes necessary for a nation to "peg" its rate of exchange, the rate at which one currency exchanges for another, at some arbitrary rate. The great depression of the 1930's was a real emergency in international trade, and the pegging of exchange rates became quite common in peacetime as well as wartime. World War II, the creation of the "iron curtain," and the Korean incident all added up to a situation demanding continued pegging of foreign exchange rates.

With the abandonment of the gold standard and the rise in strength of central banks, it seems apparent that "managed" exchange rates will continue for a long time to come, probably permanently. It has also become common to set an "order of preference" in which foreign drafts may be paid, depending on the type of commodities covered. Preference goes to everyday items with the postponement of availability of exchange for payment of imported luxury items. Persons not in possession of the necessary exchange will hesitate to order such items. It has become common for a nation to set as many as three or four rates of exchange, the less favorable rates covering the purchase of items more easily postponed.

Arrangements are often made between two central banks whereby each honors the daily drafts of its own national businessmen with periodical settlements between the two banks. Such an arrangement is likely to mean that one of the countries is chronically short of exchange and of gold. Loans become necessary in such instances and are arranged between the governments, but the bank daily settlements between importers and exporters are carried out on schedule.

The only recourse the buyer has against an improperly pegged exchange rate is to refuse to buy those foreign goods. When the set rate is an overvalued one, trade slackens and a black market in exchange appears. The rates quoted therein are more nearly at their commodity exchange value, value based on the number of hours of labor required to produce an article plus factory overhead and the cost of raw materials.

There is a minor and secondary market for foreign exchange that is conducted openly and legally but nevertheless unofficially. Tourists may bring home foreign currencies in small amounts and sometimes nationals take more money on a foreign trip than is legally permitted. These currencies are sold to a foreign trader for what they will bring. Since the amounts are relatively small, their only use is to make them available to a traveler going into the country to which the currency belongs. If exchange regulations are very strict, the buyer will have to smuggle the currency into the country.

INTERNATIONAL ECONOMIC INSTITUTIONS

The Bretton Woods Conference of July 1944 set up two new and very important international institutions for postwar use: the International Monetary Fund and the International Bank for Reconstruction and Development. The conference was attended by representatives of the allied nations, and the role of the United States was an important one. Both institutions have served well, under the auspices of the United Nations, but the peacetime conditions under which they were organized to operate have not been realized.

International Monetary Fund. The International Monetary Fund is a pool of gold and national currencies contributed, on a quota basis, by its member nations. It is a fund to stabilize the currency and exchange rates of its members. Any member may borrow under stipulated conditions, fees, and penalties, any currency which it needs to settle existing international transactions. The idea behind the Fund is the conviction that imbalances in international trade are temporary or short run and will adjust over a longer period. Fluctuations in daily exchange rates to accommodate current situations are thus minimized. Continued national borrowing may mean the exchange ratio is incorrect and requires adjustment. Minor changes in ratios may be made at will by the country concerned but major changes require consultation with the Fund.

The Fund began operations 1 March 1947. The realignment of the trade of iron curtain countries and the unsettled international conditions following World War II have not permitted a return to free or full convertibility of national currencies. Most countries have had to continue their emergency exchange controls. The Fund has not been tested under full convertibility.

International Bank for Reconstruction and Development. The International Bank for Reconstruction and Development, which started operations in June 1946, has done a great deal to increase international investments, especially in areas of low industrial levels. The guarantee of the government of the nation receiving a loan is required. It is not intended that a loan should cover a task that would be undertaken by private investment. The Bank has a total capital of about $9 billion with a mechanism for extending it if necessary. The projects undertaken to date have turned out well, and early repayment of loans is common. It is interesting to conjecture what demands might have been made on the Bank had it not been for the loan and technical-assistance programs of the United States.

Bank for International Settlements. The Bank for International Settlements (BIS) was set up under the League of Nations largely to handle World War I reparations payments and loan repayment programs. It continued in some sort of fashion during World War II. Its liquidation was assumed under the Bretton Woods programs, but such a liquidation program was never formalized. When the European Payments Union was set up, the BIS became its banking functionary.

General Agreement on Tariffs and Trade. Work on developing an international trade agreement or charter covering trading relations between nations began on the part of the United States before the close of the war and continued steadily. The United States assumed the task after its formation. Such a charter would have two objectives: (a) the elimination or reduction of specific trade barriers by national states and (b) a code of trading relations by international agreement.

The General Agreement on Tariffs and Trade (GATT), an international arrangement pending the completion of a formal charter, was set up on the initiative of the United States at a meeting of 23 countries at Geneva in 1947 to consider tariff reductions. This agreement covers many of the points in the proposed charter for international trade, long under consideration. Agreement on the Charter for an International Trade Organization was reached at Havana in March 1948, but it was never fully ratified. In the meantime the GATT continues in full force and effect. Changes have been made at subsequent conferences, the latest occurring in the spring of 1955. The United States participates in these tariff conferences under authority contained in the Reciprocal Trade Agreements Program. About 50 countries now take part. Many feel that the interests of the United States are better served under the provisions of GATT, since not as many protective exceptions are incorporated as were proposed in the Charter.

UNITED STATES FOREIGN ECONOMIC POLICY

Official postwar commercial policy of the United States favors, with regard to the other nations of the Free World, such principles as multilateralism, nondiscriminatory trade practices, reduction of trade barriers, and free competition. In currently championing a liberal trade philosophy, the United States has assumed the role that Britain played before the First World War. The policy has been opposed and partly blocked by domestic economic interests which feel that they are adversely affected.

The United States has made notable financial efforts to stabilize the Free World since World War II. The lend-lease settlements were generous to the borrowers. In 1946 we lent Great Britain $4.4 billion, which gave her a dollar credit line in the United States of $3.75 billion, with the remaining $650 million applied to the final settlement of British lend-lease obligations. A grace period of 5 years was set up after which annual installment payments on a 50 year basis began. With considerable limitations the British agreed to allow countries in the sterling area to convert their pounds sterling into dollars. Carrying out this agreement reduced irritations connected with blocked currencies. The American Government established the Export-Import Bank of Washington as its financial agent to manage many foreign trade and lending programs. The work of the Bank has been steadily enlarged and its capital expanded again and again.

The Marshall Plan. Destruction of industry, disruption of trade, and lack of capital prevented the establishment of a balanced European economy at the end of World War II. Poor crops intensified the problem in 1947. The European balance of payments with the United States showed a deficit in 1947, running at the rate of $10 billion a year. In his speech of 5 June 1947, Secretary of State George Marshall proposed a European-sponsored program including foreign aid to and self-help and mutual assistance among European countries. Sixteen countries organized the Committee of European Economic Cooperation in September 1947. They looked forward to a freer flow of goods and labor as well as a fuller use of the group's own resources. In April 1948 the Economic Cooperation Act was passed by the United States Congress to furnish means to cover essential import needs for commodities and equipment of the participating countries and to support measures of self-help and mutual aid to achieve recovery. The Economic Cooperation Administration (ECA) operated the program which provided $10 billion in grants and credits by the middle of 1951. It cooperated closely with the Organization for European Economic Cooperation, which had been formalized in April 1948. ECA became the Mutual Security Agency in December 1951, to be succeeded by the Foreign Operations Administration in 1953, and by the Internal Cooperation Administration in June 1955. Industrial production for Western Europe rose 45 percent between 1947 and 1950, exports were up 91 percent for all countries combined for the same period, and the 1950–51 agricultural output of Western European exceeded the prewar average. The United States also found it necessary to contribute to the expanding of rearmament facilities for Europe and to provide aid to China and Korea.

Program for underdeveloped areas. In the January 1949 inaugural address, President Truman introduced a fourth point to the international policy of the United States—to "embark on a bold new program for making the benefits of our scientific progress available for the improvement and growth of underdeveloped areas." He emphasized the fostering of international investment facilities and equipment which would be utilized by skills and techniques to be developed through technical assistance.

Prior to the inauguration of the Point-Four Program in 1950, technical assistance provided by the United States to Latin America arose through operations of the Coordinator of Inter-American Affairs and several subsidiary corporations. These activities were then taken over by the Institute of Inter-American Affairs, a corporate subsidiary within the Department of State. Wartime and postwar grant aid to these countries reached $88 million by the end of 1951, when the annual amounts declined. The United States Department of Agriculture provided $55 million to pay indemnities for slaughtered cattle infected and exposed to hoof and mouth disease in the 1946 Mexican outbreak. Additional sums went to pay American personnel working in Mexico to combat the disease. More than 60 million American dollars were spent for frozen beef and canned meat from Mexico. The Department of Agriculture sold this meat to foreign countries or otherwise disposed of it in foreign aid programs.

THE FUTURE

The rebuilding of flourishing international private investment is dependent on the reestablishment of currency convertibility and upon the assurances that property will not be confiscated and that earnings may be fully exported. It has been proposed that private capital from America be encouraged to flow to foreign fields by tax exemptions and by guarantees that dollars will be available for the transfer of profits back to the United States. Some relief from double income taxes on dividends earned abroad has been accomplished.

XIII
ECONOMIC PROBLEMS OF WAR AND DEFENSE PROGRAMS[1]

GENERAL

All war and defense programs have their economic aspects, for they require the use of economic resources. This was true even in the earliest times when war was far simpler and more limited than it is today. Men for the Armed Forces had to be diverted from the production of goods and services for civilian purposes or from their enjoyment of leisure, and some part of the remaining productive power had to be devoted to building ships and fortresses, to supplying provisions to the troops, and to making the simple weapons then employed. In other words, various military uses competed with each other and with civilian needs for the limited supply of manpower and other productive resources. In general, however, the proportion of total productive power used for defense and war was very much smaller in those early periods. Armies were but a small part of the population, and the technology of war was simple. The fighting men needed little equipment and supplies beyond food, clothing, horses, ships, and relatively inexpensive weapons.

With scientific development and industrialization, the economic requirements of defense and war have grown tremendously, especially during the past century. The size of wartime military hordes has increased greatly, not only absolutely but also as a percentage of the population. But a far greater cause of the increased economic requirements of war has been the revolution in military technology, which has been a part of the broad scientific and technological revolution of the modern period.

Nations have learned how to devise, manufacture, and use increasingly huge amounts of equipment to enhance the defense and offensive efforts of their Armed Forces. Older types of equipment have been improved and employed in increased quantities while countless new types of equipment have been invented, developed, and put into use. This point is emphasized by a comparison of the technology of the American Revolution with that of World War II, which saw the use of huge navies, including ships ranging all the way from landing craft to giant battleships and aircraft carriers; swarms of fighter,

[1] The material in this chapter is taken from Lester V. Chandler, and Donald H. Wallace, *Economic Mobilization and Stabilization* (New York: Henry Holt and Co., Inc., 1951), pp. 3-16, by Professor Chandler, Gordon S. Rentschler, Professor of Economics, Princeton University. The material is used by permission of the publisher.

bomber, torpedo, reconnaissance, and transport aircraft; great numbers of mobile artillery, tanks, and tank destroyers; fleets of motorized transport vehicles; millions of rifles and machine guns of great firepower; enormous tonnages of bombs, torpedoes, rockets, and shells, and many other types of offensive and defensive equipment; and huge amounts of fuel and other supplies to keep the war machine in operation. Now, more than ever before, the military advantage lies with those nations that can amass and bring into timely use the greatest amount of the most effective military equipment and supplies. Moreover, under modern military technology there is almost no limit to the amount of manpower, equipment, and supplies that can be used to some advantage for military purposes.

Because of these facts, the magnitude of war demands on a nation's economic system now is far greater than ever before. At the very time that large numbers of men and women are diverted into the military forces, a large part of the nation's remaining productive power must be used for producing military rather than civilian goods and services. It is here that a defense program, even in a rich country, encounters a stark, inescapable economic fact—the fact of scarcity. Not even in peacetime and in the absence of a military program has any economic system been able to produce enough goods and services to satisfy all the wants of all the people. Even less in time of war or preparedness can the system provide all the manpower, equipment, and supplies that would be useful for military purposes and at the same time satisfy all civilian wants. Given the fact that it cannot have all the military and all the civilian goods that it wants, a nation faces the problem of balancing its various demands against each other. It must somehow decide what part of total output will be used for military purposes and what part for civilian uses, keeping in mind the fact that more for one use necessarily means less for the other, except to the extent that the total can be expanded. At the same time the specific types and quantities of goods and services to be produced within the broad categories of military and civilian supplies must also be determined. For example, with respect to civilian goods the following kinds of problems must be solved. What part of the productive resources allocated to civilian use shall be employed to turn out consumer goods and what part to maintain and increase the stock of capital goods? What specific types and quantities of capital goods should be produced? How much of each specific type of consumer goods? How should the limited supply of consumer goods be divided among the various economic groups?

The division of military output among its many alternative uses also involves difficult decisions. The resources that can be made available to the military are rarely, if ever, sufficient to provide enough of everything that would be useful for offensive or defensive purposes. It is therefore necessary to balance the many military demands against each other in order to get maximum results, taking into consideration the types and quantities of available resources and the probable strategy and tactics of the enemy. The following kinds of alternatives must be considered:

1. *More finished military goods quickly versus more in the future.* This is practically the same problem as "armament in width versus armament in depth." In later as well as earlier stages of an armament program, a nation must decide what part of its resources devoted to military purposes will be used to produce a stockpile of finished military goods and what part will be used to build up capacity to produce more military goods at a later date. At one extreme, a nation may decide to concentrate on stockpiling finished military goods and to use none of its resources to build up its capacity to produce more of these goods later. This policy may be appropriate if the nation expects to wage a "lightning war" which will be successfully completed in a very short period of time. Such a policy is, however, subject to two dangers. In the first place, many war goods rapidly become obsolete; and in the second place, the nation is left in a vulnerable position if its "Blitzkreig" fails. At the other extreme, a nation may decide against stockpiling any finished military goods and concentrate on stockpiling raw materials and building up its capacity to produce more goods at a later date. In practice, the decision is usually a compromise between these two extremes, the proportions of available resources devoted to each of these purposes being determined by many considerations.

2. *The size of the fighting forces versus the amount of military equipment and supplies.* The available manpower may be used in varying proportions as military personnel or as workers producing war goods or expanding capacity for war goods. These uses obviously compete with each other. It is therefore necessary to balance the various uses against each other and to arrive at an "optimum" balance.

3. *The various types of military personnel, equipment, and supplies versus each other.* Competition among the various possible uses of available military resources has often been dramatized by the conflicting demands of the Army, Navy, and Air Force. But the problem is much broader. Faced with the fact that they cannot have all they want of everything, all branches of the military establishment must strive for an optimum balance among the various possible uses of personnel and supplies. They must try to avoid a relative undersupply of some things and a relative oversupply of others.

The complexity of the economic problem of supplying goods and services for rapid mobilization and war purposes stems not only from the huge size of these requirements but also from the differences between civilian and military goods and from the rapidity with which production must be shifted to meet military demands. Before the initiation of an expanded defense program, the economy is usually geared to meet the pattern of civilian demands. The locations of the various types of industries, the capacity of each industry, the types of existing specialized machinery and other productive facilities, the geographic and occupational distribution of labor, and the skills of workers are all largely determined by the pattern of civilian demands for the various types of products. This pattern must be changed greatly and rapidly as military requirements rise.

The conversion from civilian to military output is relatively simple in those cases where military goods are the same as, or very similar to, civilian goods, so that existing facilities and skills can be used to make them. Examples of this sort are military clothing and basic foods. But the problems of conversion are far more complex where, in order to meet military as well as essential civilian needs, it is necessary to expand greatly the production of a given type of product and where the pattern of military demands differs markedly from the earlier civilian pattern. For example, rapid mobilization or war requires a tremendous expansion in the output of planes, tanks, guns, ships, explosives, electronic devices, industrial alcohol, aviation gasoline, steel, copper, and so on. To adjust production to such a greatly changed pattern of demand it is necessary to convert specialized existing plants to military output, to build new facilities, to find larger amounts of many raw materials, to shift large numbers of workers from one industry to another and from one geographic area to another, and to increase greatly the number of people with certain types of skills. Moreover, this conversion of a large part of the productive power of the nation to military purposes must usually be accomplished in a minimum period of time. The security of the nation and the success of its military effort will depend largely upon the speed of the conversion.

In short, the economic problems of mobilization and war stem not only from the huge absolute size of military requirements but also from the necessity of converting productive factors and output from a peacetime to a military pattern of demand and from the speed with which this conversion must be accomplished. The economic problems of mobilization would be quite different if conversion could occur leisurely over several decades instead of being concentrated in a short period.

The preceding paragraphs emphasized two basic facts: (1) That available real resources are insufficient to satisfy all military and civilian wants, so that a nation must inevitably face and somehow solve the difficult problem of allocating its limited output and resources among the various competing military and civilian uses and (2) that in the last analysis, military and civilian wants can be satisfied only with real goods and services and not with money.

This raises another basic question: What are the sources of the goods and services available to a nation for satisfying its civilian and military wants during any specified period? The supply of goods and services to satisfy civilian and military needs is made up of three parts: (1) the nation's current output or production of goods and services; (2) the nation's inventory or stockpile of raw materials, semifinished goods, and finished goods existing at the beginning of the period; and (3) any net excess of the nation's imports of goods and services over its exports during the period. The first two sources are largely self-explanatory, the third requires further discussion.

A nation's military program can, of course, benefit by foreign trade even though the nation exports as much as it imports. It may export less essential and lower-cost goods in exchange for more essential goods which would have a higher real cost at home. Examples of such imports for the United States are rubber, tin, manganese, and so on. But the nation may also find it advantageous to import more than it exports, if this is not prevented by enemy blockades or by the diplomatic and commercial policies of other countries. The nation may secure an excess of imports over exports in the following ways: (1) It may capture, confiscate, or obtain voluntary gifts. It may capture useful equipment and supplies from the enemy; it may confiscate supplies from the enemy or from others without compensation; or it may receive gifts from allied or friendly nations. The common characteristic of these methods is that they enable a country to acquire supplies without either current or future payment. (2) It may sell assets to other countries or borrow from them. A nation may finance an excess of current imports by exporting to others a part of its stock of gold and silver; by selling to others a part of its accumulated holdings of claims against other countries (such as balances abroad, foreign stocks, and foreign bonds); or by borrowing abroad. The common characteristic of these methods is that they deteriorate a nation's international capital position; they decrease a nation's holdings of claims against other countries, or increase other countries' claims against it.

The above facts concerning a nation's sources of goods and services during any given period can be put in the form of a simple equation, as follows:

Sources of goods and services used by a nation during a given period		*Utilization of goods and services by a nation during a given period*
1. The nation's output during the period.		1. Goods and services utilized for military purposes, including amounts used to expand military capacity.
2. The net decrease of inventories during the period.		2. Goods and services utilized for civilian purposes— *a.* for civilian consumption. *b.* for maintaining and increasing the stock of capital goods.
3. Net imports during the period.		
TOTAL SOURCES	=	TOTAL UTILIZATION

The left side of the equation shows the total supply of goods and services utilized during a period, and the right side shows how they were utilized. The two sides of the equation must, of course, be equal. This equation can be used to analyze the amount of goods and services that can be made available for military use during a period. This is equal to the total amount of goods and services made available for all uses minus the amount used for civilian purposes. The amount devoted to military purposes can therefore be increased by increasing the total supply, or by reducing the amount made available for civilian use, or by both. On the side of total supply, it is often possible to expand total output above the preceding peacetime level, especially if mobilization begins in a period of business depression, widespread unemployment, and underutilization of productive facilities. Unemployed people may be put to work; the labor force may be expanded by withdrawing people from schools, housewifery, retirement, or leisure; hours may be lengthened, and work speeded up; factories and other facilities may operate extra shifts, longer hours, and at a higher tempo; and improved techniques may be introduced. It may also be possible to make more military goods available by drawing down accumulated inventories and by importing in excess of current exports. To the extent that it is possible to expand the total supply of goods and services through expanded production, drawing down inventories, or increasing net imports, it is possible to meet the expanding requirements of a military program without actually reducing the supply made available for civilian purposes. But any expansion of current military requirements in excess of the increase in the total supply must be at the expense of the amount currently made available for civilian purposes. To this extent there must be a reduction in the current supply of civilian consumer goods, or in the amount of resources devoted to maintaining or expanding the stock of capital goods, or both.

ECONOMIC CONTROLS IN A DEFENSE OR WAR ECONOMY

The preceding pages outlined some of the basic economic problems of a defense or war economy. They described the sources of goods and services available for military and civilian uses and emphasized that these are never sufficient to meet all military and all civilian wants. It is because of the inescapable fact of scarcity that a nation must face the difficult problems of "economic control." There must be control over the total amounts of goods and services produced, imported, and added to or taken out of inventories; control of the allocation of productive resources among their many alternative uses; control of the composition of output and its utilization; control of the prices of goods and services; control of wages; and so on. All these processes require human direction or control. These include Government orders prohibiting or limiting the output of some end products in order to divert production to other things; orders prohibiting or limiting the use of especially scarce materials—such as tin, rubber, or copper—in some end products in order to divert them to more essential uses; priority regulations and allocations to channel materials into specified uses; measures to channel labor into particular uses; Government directives ordering the production and delivery of specific types of products; Government rationing of consumer goods; direct limitations on prices and wages; and so on.

Direct governmental controls are not, of course, the only type of economic controls that can be employed. In peacetime, the United States and some other countries rely largely on a type of control system that is variously known as "a free enterprise system," "a competitive system," "a price system," or "a market system." The outstanding characteristic of such a system is that the Government keeps its direct controls at a minimum and relies on market forces to regulate the processes of production and distribution. Rivalry in the marketplace among buyers and sellers is allowed to regulate total output, determine the composition of output and its distribution among its many possible uses, and regulate price and wage relationships.

Some believe that even in a defense or war economy a nation should rely largely, if not completely, on market forces rather than direct governmental controls. In broad outline, competitive controls would work as follows: The Government would keep its direct controls to a minimum and would try to regulate production and distribution indirectly by controlling the effective money demand for goods and services. To divert production from civilian to military purposes, it would hold down or actually decrease total civilian spending power and at the same time it would increase its own demand for the things that it wanted. It would hold down civilian spending power in line with the quantity of goods that could be made available for civilian use by heavy taxation, borrowing, and restrictive monetary policies. Civilians would be free to spend their remaining purchasing power as they saw fit, but the total amount of purchasing power at their disposal would be limited by various fiscal and monetary controls. At the same time, the Government would increase its demand for the various things that it wanted. This would in two ways shift resources to meet the Government's requirements. In the first place, it would divert production from products with a decreased demand to products with an increased demand. Business firms would discontinue or at least reduce their output of the products whose demand had actually fallen or had risen but little and would expand their output of the products whose demand had risen most. The incentive to make these shifts would emanate from the higher profit to be made by shifting from products with a lesser demand to products with an increased demand. In the second place, the shifts of demand would automatically ration the available output and reduce civilian use of the products most in demand by the Government. The prices of those products most in demand by the Government would rise relative to other prices, and this would cause civilians to use less of them and to use their limited purchasing power to purchase things less urgently needed by the Government.

Several advantages are claimed for competitive controls. (1) They obviate the need for a large controlling bureaucracy and for governmental orders that may lead to inefficiency. (2) They preserve freedom of civilians to dispose of their limited incomes as they see fit. (3) They decrease the danger of continuing a centrally controlled economy after the return to peace.

One of the major problems in a defense or war economy is that of deciding the extent to which competitive controls will be employed and the extent to which they will be supplemented or replaced by direct governmental controls. Competitive controls do have many advantages. During a slow mobilization or a limited defense program with stable requirements, competitive controls may by themselves yield acceptable results. Even during an all-out war there may be areas in which competitive controls are most appropriate. Nevertheless, there are several characteristics of a mobilization or war economy that may make imperative the use of direct controls, even though competitive controls are most appropriate in normal peacetime periods. One of these is the great and rapid shift necessary in resource allocation. In normal peacetime periods there are, of course, continuous shifts in the allocation of resources reflecting changes in consumers' tastes, the introduction of new products, and changes in techniques of production. But such changes are usually rather slow and do not in a short period involve any large part of the nation's total output or productive capacity. Readjustments may therefore be quite gradual and limited in scope, and tardy readjustments will be tolerated. Conditions are far different during rapid mobilization or war. At such times a large part, perhaps 40 percent or even more, of the nation's output and productive resources must be diverted to military purposes, and the nature of output must change markedly. The output of many types of civilian goods has to be sharply reduced or completely discontinued, while the output of numerous categories of military goods rises manyfold. This necessitates the conversion of existing facilities to types of products they had not previously made, the creation of new facilities, and large occupational and geographic shifts of workers. These great adjustments must be made in a minimum period of time—undue delays that endanger national security, military success, and the lives of troops and civilians cannot be tolerated. Even though competitive controls are quite efficient in effecting small and gradual shifts of resources, there is no reason to believe that they would yield acceptable results when a very large part of the nation's productive capacity must be shifted in a minimum period of time.

Another difficulty of securing a sufficiently rapid shift of resources without the use of direct Government controls is found in the temporary nature of the enlarged military demands. When buyers' demands shift in a peacetime period, there is usually some presumption that the new demand pattern will persist for some time. Enterprisers and workers are therefore relatively willing to shift to those products whose demand has increased. But this is usually not true of large increases in military demands. It is usually impossible to forecast how long a war or defense program will last, but there is a presumption that it will come to an end within a relatively short period. This temporary nature of the enlarged military demands tends to inhibit in several ways the shift of production to military purposes. Enterprisers may insist on continuing to produce civilian goods, even though they actually lose money or make less than they could on military output, in order to keep their products before the public and protect their good will and their share of the civilian market. They may be reluctant to construct new facilities which will be obsolete when military demands recede. Workers may be reluctant to leave steady jobs and sacrifice seniority rights to take temporary war jobs. To overcome quickly the many obstacles of this type, the Government may have to take direct action to limit the production of certain types of civilian goods and to force production of military and essential civilian goods. Moreover, the Government may itself assume the risks of financing new facilities of doubtful postwar value.

Another obstacle to reliance on competitive controls is the great difficulty of maintaining adequate monetary incentives, while at the same time preventing inflation and avoiding an excessive amount of controversy over the distribution of income both before and after taxes. (1) It may be politically impossible to increase taxes enough to prevent very serious inflation, if direct controls over prices and wages are not employed and if money incentives are used to regulate production. (2) A tax program strong enough to prevent inflation may lessen the incentive to produce and to shift production into the desired channels. (3) Even though taxes are heavy enough to hold civilian spending power within appropriate limits, civilians may still bid some critical materials away from essential military purposes. For example, some civilians might continue to buy automobiles no matter how high their price, thereby weakening the military effort. (4) Reliance on competitive controls and monetary incentives is likely to bring about great changes in the distribution of money incomes after taxes. Such a policy is almost sure to meet widespread opposition from those who consider it immoral for some parts of the population to profit greatly from a national emergency when the nation's security is at stake and members of the Armed Forces are risking their lives. It is therefore likely to lower national morale, to evoke bitter strikes and other controversies, to interfere with production, and to set off a wage-price spiral.

This is not by any means a complete list of the difficulties involved in relying largely or exclusively on competitive controls and monetary incentives during an all-out war or a rapidly expanding defense program. It does, however, indicate why a nation may during a war or defense program elect to employ many types of direct controls which it would consider inappropriate in a normal peacetime period.

FISCAL AND CREDIT POLICIES DURING DEFENSE AND WAR

Earlier paragraphs described briefly some of the real problems of a war or defense economy—the problems of acquiring real goods and services with which to meet military and civilian needs and of allocating them among their many alternative uses. But military programs also have their financial aspects. The most obvious financial problem is that of supplying the Government with enough money to pay for all the goods and services that can be made available for its purposes. Adequacy of yield is a prime requisite of financial policy. This requirement can be met in various ways, including many combinations of taxes, borrowing, and the creation of new money by the Government itself, by the central bank, and by the commercial banking system. The real problem of financial policy is not merely to raise enough money to cover Government expenditures, but to raise this money in such a way as to facilitate the functioning of the economy and to avoid undue damage to the economy itself and to the various groups in it. Among the other important objectives of financial policy are the following: (1) Protection of production incentives. Some financial policies, such as those requiring extremely high tax rates on income resulting from desirable economic activities or those producing a galloping inflation, may seriously impair efficiency and productivity. (2) Facilitating the shift of output from civilian to military uses. Financial policies which hold down or reduce private spending power can facilitate this process of shifting production to military goods, while financing policies that continuously add to private spending power may impede it. (3) Equitable distribution of both the real and money costs of the war among the various groups in the nation. And (4) preventing inflation, or at least limiting its extent, both during and following the military effort. The prevention of inflation is desirable in order to avoid an inequitable distribution of the costs of the war, to maintain morale and avoid excessive controversy over the distribution of wealth and income, and to avoid interference with production.

PRICE AND WAGE STABILIZATION

As indicated earlier, full-scale wars and rapidly expanding mobilization programs are almost always accompanied by the generation of very serious inflationary pressures. The great increase of Government requirements generates inflationary pressures in three principal ways. (1) The rise of Government expenditures directly increases the effective money demand for output. (2) This rise adds to private money incomes and spending power at the very time that the increase of Government requirements necessitates holding down the supply of goods and services available for private purchase. And (3) increased Government requirements create fears of shortages and price increases, thereby making individuals and business firms increasingly willing to buy. The result is a strong sellers' market for both output and labor. The general tendency is to bid up prices and wages in a spiraling fashion. If the process is not halted by some sort of stabilization program, prices are likely to rise continuously throughout the war, with the usual deleterious effects on the distribution of wealth and income, on public morale, and on production incentives and the production pattern.

A workable price and wage stabilization program is therefore an essential part of a satisfactory wartime economic policy. There are two broad methods of preventing or limiting increases in the general levels of prices and wages. The first is indirect fiscal and monetary controls. These controls are not designed to place direct limitations on specific prices or specific wage rates, but to operate indirectly by limiting total spendings for output and labor. In principle, it should be possible to control total spendings for output and labor (and thereby check inflation of prices and wages) through heavy taxation that would restrict private spendable incomes and through restrictive monetary policies that would limit the supply of credit and money available for spending. In practice, however, fiscal and monetary policies are almost never restrictive enough to prevent the creation of serious inflationary pressures during rapid mobilization or full-scale war. More direct controls are therefore employed to halt, or at least to slow down, the wage-price spiral. The second method is direct controls over prices and wages. These are direct limitations on the rise of specific prices and specific wage rates, and are often referred to as wage and price ceilings. They cannot by themselves prevent the creation of some inflationary pressures, if fiscal and monetary policies are insufficiently restrictive, but they can often prevent these inflationary pressures from setting off an explosive wage-price spiral.

BIBLIOGRAPHY

Baumol, William J., and Chandler, Lester V., *Economic Processes and Policies*, New York, Harper, 1954.

Burns, Arthur E., Neal, Alfred C., and Watson, D. S., *Modern Economics*, 2nd ed., New York, Harcourt, Brace, and Co., 1951.

Chandler, Lester V., and Wallace, Donald H., *Economic Mobilization and Stabilization*, New York, Henry Holt and Co., 1951.

James, Clifford L., *Principles of Economics*, (Summary of Fundamentals with Final Examination and Answers.), 9th ed New York, Barnes and Noble, 1954.

Kiekhofer, William H., *Economic Principles, Problems, and Policies*, 4th ed., New York, Century-Crofts, 1951.

Samuelson, P. A., *Economics, and Introductory Analysis*, 3rd ed., New York, McGraw-Hill Book Co., 1955.

Economic Indicators (Monthly), Washington, D. C., Government Printing Office

INDEX

☆ U.S. GOVERNMENT PRINTING OFFICE: 1960 O - 542691